9.95
5.00

FOR MENORL

CONFESSIONS
OF A DISLOYAL
EUROPEAN

CONFESSIONS
OF A DISLOYAL
EUROPEAN

JAN MYRDAL

LAKE VIEW PRESS

CHICAGO

Lake View Press
P. O. Box 578279, Chicago, IL 60657

Library of Congress Catalog Card Number: 90-62997
ISBN   0 941702-27-8
        0-941702-26-X (pbk.)

INTRODUCTION

This is a book about a generation of European intellectuals. But it is so in two ways. It is a book about my generation. We who grew up during the thirties and were forced to consciousness during the Second World War. It was written when hindsight became possible and as the larger pattern was becoming visible. I was thirty-three when I started writing it in January 1961. I finished it in June 1967 just before I became forty.

Then when it was published it became a book for the generation that then was being forced to consciousness during the Vietnam War. The intellectuals of that generation now are at that point in their life where I was in 1967 as I finished the typescript, they are reaching forty and crossing the threshold to the age when hindsight becomes possible.

These *Confessions of a Disloyal European* are not an autobiography; neither are they fiction. I don't confess. I write. But I write in the first person singular. I use material out of my own life to make the general pattern more visible. It is like weaving. The warp is there, it is given. The weft is mine. I take the color I need to create the pattern. You could say that in doing this I am writing inside a specific Nordic literary tradition that lacks regard for any privacy. So did Strindberg. So do all of us. As we don't suffer under the strange literary convention that tells you to disguise people and hide their faces, I can use any thread I find necessary for the pattern. By using my individual experiences without falsifying them with what is called good taste I wanted to lift our common experiences into consciousness, and thus make the European intellectual as a type clearly visible.

When I woke up the night was deep around me. I switched on the bed lamp and could see the second hand of the clock throbbing forth time. 05:28, a winter morning. The snow was beating against the windows, stubbornly hammering the panes. And during this brief moment before the pain started I noticed that I had woken up in the middle of a plea for the defence. The outline of the dream, its pictures, symbols and content, had already sunk back but the trial had continued this night too. I had spoken for my right to live. Tried to prove to myself that what I was doing also gave me the right to exist.

I lay quite still in the light. Words formed themselves slowly in my thought-stream. The second hand was moving forward and the snow was scratching against the glass. Then the pains started. I had been expecting them. I tried to turn between the sheets, turn away from the pains. But knew that it was useless. The brown glass bottle with pills stood on the table just beside the clock. The pills are silver-coloured. They erase the pain. But at the same time they make me weak and take away my strength. If I take so many pills that the pains are all gone, then I hardly can walk to the bathroom without aid. And my thoughts wander in mist. My anxiety in a drugged condition when I feel myself unable to think clearly is stronger than my aversion to pain. During the last two months I have only taken three pills. Even though the prescription says that I am supposed to take two pills three times daily. If I did that, then I would move around in a mental dusk all the time. And the pills don't heal, they only lessen the pain. Thus the question of taking or not taking the pills is not a medical question. Neither is it just a question of my anxiety when I feel I am losing my grip on my life and my thoughts. It is a moral question. As a thinking and working individual I can face myself—defend my existence; drugged, I can see no justification for my existence. Suddenly I am in great pain and I notice that I am thinking:

—If only they healed, then it would be my right to take them. This weakness irritates me. I know they don't heal. I get out of bed. The deerskin fell under my bare feet.

When I have been to the bathroom, washed, shaved and dressed, I go down to the kitchen. I pour coffee from the thermos bottle and make a sandwich. Still the night is heavy outside the windows. Whirls of snow slowly turning. The kitchen lamp lights up the snow and as I sit at the table I can hear the snow grinding on the other side of the black windowpane to my left. When I turn towards the sound I can see myself, the cup of coffee, the table, the kitchen lamp, and through this a grinding white whorl of snow in the night.

I have pains all the time and it is difficult to sit still. I feel that I want to go to the library, lie down on the blue couch and read. I walk through the library into the study, turn on the desk lamp with the green shade, put paper into the typewriter and start writing. As I write the night becomes lighter and a new day is coming. A day like any other day.

.   .   .   .

The pains are very intense today. They come in wave upon wave with short intervals. They are almost as bad as when I was sitting in Peking and writing out my report from Liu Ling village. Almost, but not quite, because then I could only sit typing ten minutes at a time before I was forced to lie down and recover my breath. I speak about them just now because they evidently play a part in my situation today. I am also convinced that they are partly a product of the conflict I am living through, at the same time as they help bring this conflict into relief, all the time keeping open the door to escape. Escape into physical pain.

The doctors, and I too, are convinced that the pains are not—at least not just now, and as far as one can judge them —the symptoms of an imminent death. The apostle speaks about a thorn in the flesh. That is, he does so in the modern (1917) Swedish version of the Bible. In the older Swedish version he spoke of a pole in the flesh. So I feel. And the many possible meanings of the expression fascinate me.

But to say that the pains also have a psychological background and that my intense feeling of conflict convulses into a shrill pain does not take away the reality of physical pain. That I am living in conflict with myself and that I carry on trials against myself during sleep could be called neurotic. But that is juggling with words. Because the conflict is real. For the same reasons that I don't want to lessen the pain by drugging the brain I don't want to avoid the conflict by giving up my insight.

The plea for the defence that I entered during my sleep and broke off by waking up should be carefully scrutinized and the trial brought to light, because I am afraid that I will judge myself innocent in a feigned verdict where the sleep-protecting function of dreaming gives me the chance to avoid clarifying my position.

But before the trial can begin and the records can be submitted I want to note down the role of this pain. Now it is receding and I hope it can keep on dulling down and then disappear. It does not make me more productive. And even if I can work despite the pain I prefer to have my periods of work undisturbed by shrilly piercing cramps. It prevents me from going to bars (which undoubtedly is good for my budget) and thus cuts the bonds to many old friends. It also stops me from holding lectures. Only with great reluctance do I accept any invitation to give a speech, lead a discussion, appear on radio or television, meet friends and acquaintances. And as the pain gives me a hunted feeling (that—as I have said—is an illusion) that time for me might be very short, it makes me impatient, even rude, to strangers. I find that these people disturb me in my work, I look at my watch and hear the seconds ticking away into nothing while I just sit. All this can be harmful. It can also distort my perspective. If my eyes turn inward and I shut myself inside past life, then my possibilities of judging the events become limited.

At the same time the pain helps me to screen off all that which is irrelevant. Thus it is a help. I can give all my time to what I find useful. I have wasted so many hours just being pleasant. Now pain helps to give me the ruthlessness I need to create peace and quiet around me so I can work. But I am fully aware that the pain, the physical processes inside my body, bind too much of my energy and take up too much of my attention. And if I once again become fully well—which I doubt—then I will be able to turn this energy that is now uselessly bound towards a more functional activity. But not just friends and talk. Not like before.

Of course the pain has made me absent-minded. It has isolated me and made me pressed for time. I have noticed that I begin to forget faces and names very quickly. He who doesn't interest me I forget. A wet sponge straight over the blackboard. Sometimes this becomes awkward. I don't any longer count on meeting them in the future, they have nothing to say to me, I forget them in order not to burden my memory with useless information. But I sometimes get a uneasy feeling that I certainly know many of those I meet in the street. It can't be normal that I can walk through Stockholm for days without ever meeting anybody I recognize. When I turn around I see that they are lifting their hats. I quickly look down and hurry on. I usually blame this on my nearsightedness. I laugh when I say this. Smile. Hope that people believe this. But I know that this too is just a defensive reaction. One which I developed as a child in order to be left in peace. The pain gives me a new excuse for not meeting others than those I choose. Though it cheats me, it lets me slip. It might be that I will soon reach a stage where I don't even see those I want to meet. There a danger, I feel.

The pain is going on its sixth year now. No longer unknown to me. And so we can begin.

I hesitated for a long time before the wording: "Confessions of a disloyal European." The word "confessions" is ambiguous. It has a religious meaning. But even if I regard my present situation as one where I "make an examination of my conscience," I mean by "confessions" more an apology than a confession.

When I finally decided to use the word it was my clear intention to place myself inside a specific intellectual tradition. The sentence has a strong associative value. And in the word "confession" I also put the meaning "acknowledgment of." Confession, in the sense in which I use the word, thus become an adherence to experiences and actions; a statement of them; a profession of the European intellectual tradition.

Had I wanted to confess, do penance, admit and sur-render, then I would have formulated the sentence differently: "A European intellectual confesses." But in my apologetic confession of an intellectual tradition, an intellectual style of living, there is no contrition. What tradition, and which style, ought by-and-by to become clear to the reader.

I thus only "confess" that which I consider necessary for the reasoning. Any attempt at a more general confession (a piece of writing where the confessing of this or that is the chief aim) becomes such a thoroughly deceitful structure of sounds that it becomes worthless. In order to be honest I must put a boundary on my honesty. If I make the boundary too wide it will include fields where I inevitably begin to lie. The lies will then contaminate all the material. Thus I censor. But I do it consciously. I choose to write what I consider important.

In no case do I tell the whole truth. Only when it concerns insignificant details do I avoid the retouching. This I do in the interest of truth.

Much bad writing could be avoided if the writers were more aware that great sincerity is deeply untruthful, makes the truth fulfil the function of rationalization. It is nude but not naked. (The nude truth.)

Of course the knife has to be guided by knowledge and insight if the whole operation is not to be a bloody mess. Have you seen a butcher carve up a pig? The knife fondling the joints. I want to work as that butcher. Not as the housewife with her knife.

Nic.

I met her in Gothenburg as the European war was ending. Her hair was short; she had been in a concentration camp. Her hair had the colour of many dyes; she had worked underground. The last time I saw her was in Oslo in 1956:

—You want to be happy? Why? You are supposed to work.

Her last letter reached me in Kabul in 1959. After that she didn't answer any letters. Coming to Scandinavia I called and asked:

—How is Nic?

—She is dead.

A decision has been reached; young H is to make a career in the social sciences. His first independent work at the university is a paper on the beginnings of the labour movement in Norrköping during the middle of the nineteenth century. The subject interests me and one day when we meet in the street I discuss it with him. During this talk I ask him if he—now that he is to place Norrköping in the stream of history—has read Marx, Engels, Lassalle.

—Not exactly read, he said. It isn't necessary. You know, at the University in Uppsala we use abstracts.

If I am living in a hot climate where the air temperature exceeds the body temperature even during night—as I am just now—and if I then drink—as last night—my dreams become vivid, colourful and cinematic. Alcohol might be the nerve-stimulating, narcotic factor which triggers off this type of dream. But the climate is decisive; the further north I move, the greyer become the colours, the more stereotyped the contents and the worse the directing of the dreams. (On the basis of this I could construct a climatological theory of literature—but I don't. I am fully aware of the fact that this is just my individual physiological reaction to heat and high humidity.)

The basic content of the dreams remains the same in

all climates. Childhood fears; fragments of daytime
work; re-enacting of long-since-forgotten conflicts. I seldom have openly sexual dreams; they are symptoms of
abstinence, release of emotional needs, and thus will not
occur when you live together with a woman you like.
(Mayakovsky once pointed out that the best love poetry,
the most convincing erotic imagery, can be written only
when the poet is not in love. The beloved one most often
finds it hard to understand that the condition for being
beautifully and lovingly described is that there is no love
any longer. In our Western culture many women, espe-
cially intellectual ones, are groomed to prefer this love.
The poetry of love instead of love itself. It also is valuable
for our social stability that our flesh is converted to words
living beyond us. Well, this was a parenthesis.)

These tropical and alcoholic dreams are colourful. The
colours are like the old Kodachrome colours. Deep blue,
"brilliant" black, strong red. Yellow and green seldom
come through well. The pictures are rigidly composed,
the perspective is bold with violent foreshortenings and
distortions (though controlled). After reading *Erfindung
des Verderbens*—reading the book as I had no chance to
see the film—the technique of constructive pictures used
in that film returned in my dreams. But they were changed
from night to night, became more colourful, fused with
my normal dream construction. The directing is strict. I
often dream the same scene five or ten times until it has
become perfect. In the retakes I move a person here,
change a colour there, recast, correct, once more recast.
I myself am seldom a main character. (Except in scenes
that are driven by a strong emotional charge—the fear of
being sexually deceived, for instance.) I have too much
to do with the directing of the play. Now and then I project
myself into the main characters and partake of their emotions, which is not very pleasant.

Some scenes are quite amusing though. Tonight I was working with a wonderful satirical military parade in Paris. The beginning was formal and stiff: the drums, the parading paratroopers and the general's salute. Then the ritual dissolving into wildest parody (partly through a change of tempo). But when I wake up and run through the night's work one fact stands out in horrifying clarity. This whole dream sequence, where the colour was so beautifully worked out, where the directing had been so careful, where the artistic conception was clear and the play based on my strongest (and most hidden) personal emotions, was a terribly sentimental dime-store novel. As literature it was lousy, as lousy as Buñuel. On this insight I build my theory of literature and literary work.

I once knew a man, a high school teacher, who during ten years was married to a woman who was regularly unfaithful two or three times a week. When these ten years had passed he suddenly sued her for divorce on the grounds of adultery. I asked him why. He answered:

—One evening my wife told me she was going to a lecture. I went to bed early and fell asleep. I woke up as a man was leaning over my bed, vomiting in my face. "Oh, I'm so sorry," he said, "I didn't know you existed." When I looked at my wrist watch it was four o'clock in the morning.

—Speaking about 1953 and all that, said a Polish intellectual, I can tell you something that happened the year after. My wife had come home to Warsaw after a fairly long vacation in the Tatra Mountains above Zakopane. My organization had a lodge there. She was pregnant. Had found another man. I was desperate. I became still more desperate when I found that she had been going around with this other man for quite some time and planned to arrange everything so that I was to be the official father and she would keep the other man. I went to the newspaper office in the morning as usual but after an hour or so I broke down and began to cry. I lay sobbing over my typewriter when the subeditor came to my room. He looked at me. Then he said, "But you are a Marxist, aren't you? Try to see what has happened dialectically!"

—But, continued my Polish friend, as you know I had lived abroad during the war. I had sat it out in a neutral country and I didn't return to Poland until 1948. But the editor, he had been in Poland the whole time. He had taken part in the resistance. He had been jailed but managed to escape. In the final stage of the war he had come to Auschwitz and only sheer chance had saved him from the gas chambers and ovens; all his family and relatives had been gassed. After the war he had taken part in the bitter and tragic political struggle. He was a Polish intellectual, a Jew and Marxist who had survived it all. Now that I was crying because my young and rather sloppy wife had slept with another man he looked at me with his big brown eyes and said:

—But you are a Marxist. Then try to see what has happened dialectically.

As a child when I lived in central Stockholm I was once playing in the doorway of another house. The caretaker saw me. When I heard him coming down the stairs I ran. He caught me in the street and started hitting me. He struck me in the face.

—I'll teach you, he said. You bastard.

Then he kicked me and left.

Close by a man was beating his Airedale terrier. A woman screamed at him:

—I will report you to the police.

I thought a lot about this the following days.

.   .   .

A gypsy family had tried to settle in the small town of
Mariefred (Peace to Mary) where I was living. The good
citizens, afraid of a drop in land prices, had tried to get
them to move. The press in Stockholm had written about
it. The citizens became afraid of scandal. Now there was
a meeting of the town council to decide what to do. Re-
luctantly it was decided that they would get a house. On
the way out from the meeting a middle-aged man turned
to me and said:

—Gypsies! One ought to get rid of people like that.

—Fine, I said. You gas them and I will heat up my
furnace.

As he was a Social Democrat, the Labour people said
after that that I was antilabour.

During the war I went to the secondary school in
Bromma. A middle-class suburb. There, for some time, I
had contact with a gang of boys from good families who
lived by the shore. We committed burglary, stripped bi-
cycles, one of us forged a bank deposit book. The criminal
activities covered only one year. No one was caught. None
of the members of the gang were suspected. Now I see
that almost all of them are solid citizens. One is a chief
engineer, one a doctor, two are teachers, one is still at the
university engaged in research (has just gone to the USA
as an atomic scientist), two are businessmen, and one is
a lawyer.

During the present campaign against juvenile delinquency the lawyer has written an article in the conservative paper. He demands energetic measures. He speaks
of the preventive effect of punishing some as examples. He
suggests hard, sharp shock.

Surely he cannot have completely blocked his ability
to remember his own juvenile delinquency. Nor is he lying.
What he writes must be his honest opinion. One good

citizen writing for his fellow citizens about a civic problem.
If he ever considers himself in relation to his opinions
he must see himself as an exception. Most likely, though,
he never established any connection between his personal
experiences and his general theories. He is thus neither
a scientist nor an artist. Just a lawyer. His honest face stares
at me from the paper. If he at least were dishonest; then
he might occasionally be struck by . . . "There but for the
grace of God go I."

He is not even aggressive. He writes calmly, factually,
logically. He is not punishing others for his own sins. And
since he is neither gifted nor dishonest he will certainly
go far and be of great harm.

In the fall of 1947 I was in love with B. She was good-
looking, intelligent and we said we thought that we had
much in common. We were going steady for some time,
but she did not allow me to sleep with her. In December
that year I left for Belgrade. When I came back to Sweden
I married another girl. In February 1949 I came to Stockholm by train from Herrljunga. Met B. Having met again
we both realized that we actually were very much in love
with each other. I followed her to her room and now she
wanted "to give herself to me," as she expressed it.

Suddenly I remembered that I had not washed my feet
for several days. There were reasons for this. I had hitchhiked up through Sweden, had spent the night at the
county jail of Herrljunga, and had been put on the train to
Stockholm. It was in the middle of winter and it was cold.

But as I was afraid that my feet stank—which would
not correspond to the image I wanted B to have of me—
I tried to find a way to escape from the situation. Unfortunately the fact that my feet (probably) stank did
not strike me until B had started to undress. I could not
find anything more convincing to say than that I seemed

to love the girl I was married to. B was very understanding and we sat for a long time talking about self, soul and love.

And all this because I had forgotten to wash my feet. Or was it?

As a souvenir of a bicycle accident as a child I have a scar on my left knee. The scar is rather large, a foot long and nearly an inch wide. The skin over the scar is thin, wrinkled and reddish. It lacks pigment. When I am suntanned and wear shorts the scar becomes very prominent.

In the summer of 1953 I—among other activities—took part in voluntary work helping to construct the "23 August" stadium in Bucharest. It was a hot and sunny summer. I worked very hard. I was mentioned in the wall newspaper as an exceptionally good worker. This spurred me further. I became lean and suntanned.

I wore what was then called a Monty outfit. Khaki shorts, khaki shirt with shoulder straps, breast pockets and short sleeves. From photos I see that I must have made an undefinable military impression.

An Italian girl named Maritza was young and beautiful in a dark and lush maner. We worked side by side. I fell in love with her. One night when we were walking under the trees along the avenue out towards the Triumphal Arch and were all alone (normally Bucharest is a town where people go to bed early) Maritza told me she loved me.

—You are so beautiful, she said, so tall and so exotically blond.

I was very surprised. But before I could say anything she leaned down, touched my scar with her fingertips and said:

—You got this while fighting as a guerrilla in your country?

—Not exactly, I said. I could not very well answer that I had tumbled off a bicycle in a Stockholm suburb. Then she kissed me and I never said anything more about the scar.

Stockholm, February 1961, early morning, rain against the windowpanes and I wake up. The morning newspapers have not come yet. Gun lies in the camp bed beside me. She sleeps on her left side, curled up, the pillow hugged in her arms. I like looking at her. It rains harder. It is never difficult to fall in love, look at a sleeping woman and feel desire or tenderness. Difficult, though, to live together with someone.

The rain continues. Morning sounds from the railroad. They are switching freight cars. Gun Khanum. Deserts and mountains and travelling together through many years and many countries. And I know that most women say that they dream about travels and deserts. Few mean what they say. And I look at her and she turns and stretches her legs and I say to myself that it is not just that she is a woman of mine there asleep, one that I am in love with, and that I look at with desire or tenderness all according to the circumstances. She is also a woman I can talk to and travel with. She has a tough endurance and a stubborn levelheadedness.

In our culture it is never difficult to fall in love. We groom our women to be attractive. They are given high heels so that they may walk as if they carried a hidden treasure under their skirts. Most of them believe they do. But that is all. It is not after coitus I get depressed. It is when I wake up and find them there next to me and they start to talk. In such moments I start believing in celibacy.

It still rains. I am going to my publisher's to discuss a new trip. I dress. Gun is awake. She has made coffee.

—I am in fact quite happy to have found you, I say.
You are rare. And after all I like you a lot.

—Now you raise a lot of money so we can travel far,
Gun says.

The scar, the one on my left knee, is actually the result
of my despair during adolescence. The spring of 1943 as
I was going to Bromma Secondary School. The days were
yellow and sticky like old glue. Sour smell of damp cloth.
No time to read and no time to study. The school stole
all my time. The long school day was a desert of hopeless-
ness. I was fifteen years old and they tried to make me
a happy homework-doer by saying that I—if I continued
to follow the schedule and answer by rote for yet another
fifteen or twenty years—with my brains would become
a Ph.D. and jump from pupil's desk to professor's chair.
Ignorant and inexperienced as I was, I saw no possibility
of breaking this vicious circle. I can still wake up at night
with a nauseous feeling, dreaming I am back in Bromma
Secondary School and have this perspective of damnation
ahead of me.

In this mood I rode my bicycle down the steep hill
under the school. In the middle of the curve I turned
myself into a mirror image. I lifted my hands from the
handlebar. I shouted:

—Möbius!

That day I had been thrown out of the classroom because I had created a disturbance. We were learning
geometry. Our mathematics teacher was old. He is dead
now. We used to call him Donald Duck. His feet were
so large. He was unmarried and smelled; he never washed.
I had tried to tell him that the whole Euclidean geometry
was false; had spoken of asymmetry and Möbius. I had
tried to prove my point by making a Möbius strip. The

whole class had laughed and I had been thrown out.
Donald Duck was beet-red in the face and his saliva
splattered over my face as he said:
—I will report you, I will report you.
That always happened when I took an interest in the
subject of the lesson. Only when I slept at my desk was
I considered a tolerable student. And the class always
laughed.

The bicycle was picking up speed. I grasped the left
handle with my right hand and the right handle with my
left hand. It is difficult to ride a bicycle on flat ground
with mirror-turned reflexes. At high speed around a curve
it is impossible. When I regained consciousness I lay with
my head on the curbstone, vomiting. My left leg lay under
the frame of the bicycle. The front wheel was twisted
into an 8.

I was taken home. Fainted. Was taken to the hospital.
Got bandaged. The leg became swollen. My pains
increased. I was taken back to the hospital, where
they performed a minor operation and put the leg in a
cast.

Now I read, just read, read whatever I wanted to read.
Through the window I could see the others going to
school in the morning and coming home in the evening.
But I was free and could read what I wanted. It was the
first bright period during all the dark school years. The
first time I had the chance to study.

But—the cast was removed. I was declared recovered
and once more brought to school. But now I found that
I could get away from school regularly by going to the
hospital in town to get my knee drained of water. I had
gotten a legal reason for nonattendance. Every second day
I went to school and every other day I went to the hospital. In reality, though, I only went to the hospital once
a week. The two other free days I spent at the city library.

The knee never troubled me much. It was somewhat swollen due to the water, but this tended to disappear and whole mornings of exercise were necessary to get it so filled with water that the clinic would agree to treat it. Now and then there was a crunching sound from the joint when I straightened out the leg and the loose meniscus locked it.

In the spring of 1944 I happened to be at the hospital. I only visited it once a month. The knee was free from water. But I still complained about the crunching sound and the loose meniscus. The doctor studied my card. In spite of everything, I had visited the hospital quite often and the card was filled with writing. He looked worried. Then he fetched the professor. The professor said:

—We can't keep on trifling with this any longer. This must be operated on.

I was operated on. The result was a long and quite painful hospitalization and a scar. The knee still crunches. The meniscus still locks it now and then.

When I got out of hospital in the spring of 1944 I did not need to use illness as a crutch any longer. I knew what I wanted and knew how I was to get away from the Bromma Secondary School.

When we, and all the world with us, were fifteen years old one of us was known for his numerous love affairs. In our own difficulties in establishing contact with the other sex we looked up to him with a certain degree of respect and admired his apparently easy handling of girls.

One day as we were talking of girls and love he said:

—I, I have taken my sex in my own hands and mould it as I like.

As we looked at him he blushed. Thereafter our interest in his love-life decreased.

· · ·

When I went to school I was always hungry for books. The authorities served us predigested ideas that I strongly suspected to be misconceptions. During that time I promised myself that my grown-up life would be organized in such a way that I would be able to read much, read whatever I wanted.

I saw the family life of the suburbanites and their loveless love-life. At the same time I had to live through the degrading abstinence of adolescence. Told myself: in my life, love won't be their love. I will never live in a dead asceticism, neither will I let myself be swindled into accepting a dull habitual married life.

Witnessed how people betrayed their convictions, how they spat in their own face, how they conformed. Promised myself not to conform, not even if I were to be given a two-car garage, a model railroad and a pat on the back.

I can cite other examples. Their order is without significance and so is the youthful pathos. The main thing is that I did get the life I wanted. But if I have managed to achieve the life, the style of living that I, as an adolescent, found true *against* everything that was told me and that I considered humanly degrading, what would have happened if I had gone to a school where I had been given intellectual freedom, if I had seen only warm, comradely sexual relationships and never seen how people betray themselves?

It is a disquieting thought.

The consequences would be inhuman.

I console myself by saying that my opinions and my outlook are of such rationality and vitality that they always would dominate even if they were socially accepted.

I know a girl who was born and grew up in one of the Balkan states. Now she is married to a Swede. One day she says:

—This Sweden where they are only able to love dogs and cats and don't like people.

A moment later her six-year-old daughter comes in; the daughter says:

—Mother! Don't sing! They can hear you! I'm so ashamed!

Four years later I am sitting with my son in a restaurant. He says:

—Don't speak so loud, father. They can hear you.

I remember the girl from the Balkans, look at my son and understand that he is growing up to be a good Swede.

Speaking about passion my friend N said:

—I was married to a girl for five years. During these five years we travelled from country to country. We seldom spent more than a couple of months at the same place. We were unfaithful to each other. We had breakups. Twice I tried to slit her throat with the kitchen knife. Once I tried to shoot myself. I told her lovers that I would shoot on sight and bought a gun. I smashed my normal existence. Lost all possibility of working. When I met her again after some years she said, "I don't think you really loved me. Being in love, you see, is to burn, to be consumed. It just can't be such a cosy, commonplace and drab marriage as ours. All your feelings have to sing when you love."

The intellectual and his role: India on New Year's Day, 1959. A Pen Club conference in Orissa. A poor and starving province of a poor and starving country. They were all there. The president, the prime minister. (Nehru was still alive; he slept during most of the speeches.) A democratic meeting where everybody paid the same, five rupees a day. For the five rupees the wellborn got a suite at the guesthouse. VIP's ate with the prime minister.

And he had a good table. The common herd of authors also paid five rupees. They got lousy lodging and lousy food; lousy even by Indian standards. Still democracy was victorious. We all paid the same. I was a Westerner so of course I was wellborn. The last day a fat Brahmin from Bombay spoke. He wrote poetry, it was said.

—In this welfare society of ours people are only interested in the material things of life. The people only talk about food and money and good living. It is our duty, the duty of the intellectuals, to get people to raise their eyes from the material to the spiritual values of life.

I had long hair in 1947. One evening in October at B's, with whom I was in love at that time, S and D suggested that I cut my hair short. B protested, but we cut my hair that evening. B collected my hair in a paper bag. Later she used it to stuff a pillow. We were in love. In the fall of 1956 I met her. We happened to live next door to each other. I asked her what had become of the pillow.

—Oh, she said, your hair became moth-eaten in 1954, so I had to throw the pillow away.

Breech Candy is a club in Bombay. The best bath and the only good swimming pool near the centre of the city. In January 1959 I see that a placard is still hanging there:

> For Europeans and persons
> of European origin
> only.
> Dogs and Indians
> not allowed.

This irritates me. I refuse to go there. That night I meet a Swede. I talk to him about this. I maintain that it is indefensible that the Indian government should still—twelve years after Independence—allow this. He looks at me and answers:

—But they have driven us away from everything we have built here in India. They have taken away everything that was ours. But at least they have the decency to let us keep this, our last reservation, to ourselves.

He was twenty-eight, had spent two months in India. Came directly from Uppsala University. They later told me he would be one of the bright young men of our Foreign Office.

I was ill and in bed for nearly half a year in 1959–1960. That was a period of intellectual inactivity. I was feeble and tired. I read Westerns, science fiction, crime. It didn't matter if I fell asleep while reading them. What were most difficult to accept—even with this blunted intelligence—were the well-written, "classic" British detective stories. They were so obviously lacking in passion. And the strange attitude that it is more normal to kill your wife than to divorce her could not be explained even by the British legal system. It all seemed very strange to me. Violence and cruelty without even sex and lust. I read about extramarital love affairs that were described as if it was a common understanding between reader and writer that men sometimes have a strange need of ejaculation for which they then need vessels. Strange.

Particularly strange since detective stories from other cultures, for instance the Latin, where divorce is still more difficult than in the Anglo-Saxon culture, manage to depict both the passion and the agony of passion. Violence there—even in bad novels—becomes fateful.

Tried to find an explanation for this. Supposed that this

literature satisfied the emotional needs of a middle-aged, middle-class group of readers whose sexual life and aggressive instincts were so muted that not even in the satisfaction of their emotional needs did they allow themselves a deviation from their code.

But R told me:

—You are quite wrong. You have never lived in England. I have. The English women are just like they are depicted in the English detective novels. It is horrible but true.

R was talking about the upper middle class. When I got better I found a box full of late-nineteenth-century pornography in the Shankar market. It had belonged to an English officer and gentleman. Most of the books were sadistic, Colonel Spanker and all those, but some items were interesting. The most thumbed books were those about defloration of very young girls.

> About three months after this he came to my house with a 3-year-old girl and asked me if I wanted to enjoy her. I said that she would surely die if I did. He just laughed and told me to watch him enjoy her. I got curious and watched them . . . his penis was very long and thick; it was thicker than the little child's arms, and almost as thick as her thighs. It was also very funny to see such a small child lying naked under such a big man . . . I could now see that if he pushed in the whole thing, the penis would come out from the back of the girl . . .

Among the other books that had belonged to this man were all the tomes about Empire and Frontier Policy. With a dream life like that, three-year-olds and conquering Afghanistan, it was not surprising that his more official fiction reading had been the classic English detective novel. I wonder how his wife looked. His son, in any case, went to public school.

I have never understood people who speak about their happy youth. Sweet sixteen and all that. All the teenagers I have met have been marked by the same social impotence. A jerky lack of power. A typical example:

I am seventeen. I have gone to the NK department store to buy underwear. When I pass the beauty parlour I see a beautiful girl. She is so beautiful that I get all dry in my throat. Smitten with passion I rush up to her. I push aside all the middle-aged women standing there. I tread on their toes. I have eyes only for the girl. She smiles. All the middle-aged women start talking as I push them away with both hands. They seem to grumble. I look into her eyes. I desperately seek for words, for a chance to make contact. Her eyes. She smiles. Suddenly I hear my voice; it croaks loudly:

—Where can I buy my pants?

Silence grows up like a brick wall around me. The smile dies. I blush, I stutter, I feel my saliva rising in my mouth, I turn and run. The shame. And all the middle-aged women who are turning, turning looking after me. Their voices rising again.

The trial of Eichmann is being reported in the press. A good and well-behaved bureaucratic murderer. I find in a Swedish newspaper at the Embassy in New Delhi that the noted businessman X is celebrating his sixtieth birthday in Gothenburg.

There is a picture of him on page 23 and some pretty words. "Well known for his social activities." I know about him. Only the purest coincidence has saved that man from the gallows. I almost feel like writing him. But I don't. It would not help. Nothing would. Eichmann with his globular bureaucratic eyes understands nothing. Neither does X.

I was in Gothenburg in the summer of 1945. There was a big fire near Järntorget. One of my journalist friends was notified by a fireman that there were "strange" things in the attic. My friend got hold of a taxi. He managed to get through the police lines and went up into the burning building. In the attic he found the archives of the Swedish Nazi party. The journalist, the fireman and the taxi driver carried the entire archives out. No one thought of delivering the material to the police. Quite the contrary. In 1945 we did not trust the police. (Sweden had been a pro-German neutral. Through the IKPK in Berlin the Swedish police had direct and regular contact with the Gestapo. The chief of police in Stockholm, Eric Ros, wrote—as representative of Sweden in the IKPK—July 23, 1940, that Sweden accepted Reinhard Heydrich as president of the IKPK. After Heydrich had been killed SS General Nebe became president; after Nebe, SS General Kaltenbrunner. The contact between the Swedish police and the Gestapo was kept up until the end of the war. Some people were fired from the force when the scandal was new. The young cabinet member who had been—partly —responsible later became prime minister. Then everything was forgotten. The people whom the Swedish police had deported from Sweden to the Gestapo were dead anyway.)

There were lists of members, there were minutes and documents. There was also a list: "Jews to annihilate; Gothenburg." X had been the man who was to be responsible for the job. He had made a thorough job. Even the names of the least well known, those who did not themselves know about their Jewishness, even those who thought themselves good reactionary Swedish bourgeois,

as well as those of the best known, all the names were
there. Jews to annihilate; Gothenburg.
Yes, X was socially active.

When I was ten I read Strindberg's *Inferno*. I liked it.
It was a book of crystal-clear lucidity. The observation
that one felt one was snapping a thread when one walked
between two people talking to each other was quite according to my own experience. Like most children I had
—partly as a game, but only partly—acquired a highly
developed magical system with which I could control
reality. The stones of the street pavement were a pattern
of joints and these joints constituted a mathematical problem; walking thus became an expression of formal logic;
one's steps built up a formula. Joints to step on, to over-
step, to double-step—and all this in a manner so un-
obtrusive that the grownups would not see and interfere.
Street corners were provided with positive or negative
charges and could be combined to cancel each other out.
Unpleasant grownups, teachers or police, would disappear in a fog if one only focussed the eyes in such a manner
that they floated away. Their words could be drowned if
one, by straining the back of the tongue, created a humming noise in the ears. Rhymes that were recited silently
with the sight—not the eyes—turned inward would render
any order or rebuff ineffective and nonexistent.

This is nothing strange. If the reader is able to remember
his own childhood he will find this memory a fascinating
study in anthropology.

Nearly twenty years later, in the winter of 1955–1956,
I happened to live at the Orfila in Paris where Strindberg
had lived through his *Inferno* period. It was a hard winter
to live through. I had to face up to my own life. Had to
make a personal decision that was hard to make. That
winter too I read *Inferno*. Found that my image of the

Hotel Orfila as well as my whole impression of Paris had been founded on the experience of the ten-year-old JM that once read *Inferno*. Through these eyes had I seen Paris the whole time I had lived there. They had guided my steps. And today when I think of *Inferno* I find myself appearing in a double exposure: walking down the Drott-ninggatan in 1937 and walking up Rue d'Assas 1956. But the strongest image is that of the ten-year-old. This is so because *Inferno* is one of the very few books written with a child's imagination.

Nice people, the ones that call themselves "ordinary" and are well brought up, scare me. When they stand silently gazing at you, you hear their prejudices tick. As our society is organized and as the consciousness of the citizens has been programmed I know that the pogroms are just under the surface in Sweden. It scares me. Let me give an example.

I had been on the waiting list for municipal housing in Stockholm since 1947. In the spring of 1954, when I had come back to Sweden and had been listed for seven years as waiting for a flat, I went to the municipal housing authority. After a long wait I was led to my place. At this desk I was to be allowed to speak to an official. He listened to me. He nodded. He disappeared for half an hour, then he came back with my card, held it up and said:

—You have been abroad. We have struck you from our list. You must understand that we Stockholmers have priority.

I—like most of those waiting for a flat—was in a desperate situation. I had to get a place to live. The rational argument that I could have used would of course have been the rights of the "Overseas Swedes." That argument, had it been used, would have led to an interesting discussion and possibly—it depends on the organizational strength of the Union of Overseas Swedes—to a formal correspondence and an impressive file. Not to a flat of course.

But the official was from Scania and spoke with a uvular R, while north of Scania Swedes use a tongue-point R. After a moment of hestitation I decided to use the power of irrationality and prejudice. If he had been a Jew I would have thought of the gas chambers and gone out and committed suicide; but he was an ordinary blond Scanian. I stood up, took two steps backward so all other desperate applicants could see me, turned up my voice to full volume and said:

—I was born in the parish of Matthew in central Stockholm. I grew up on Kungsholmen (the Royal Island). Now you say that "we Stockholmers" have priority. You say that! You Scanian!

People gather. They come walking. They look. A crowd is formed. And they all are desperate. The official becomes nervous. He disappears again. I remain standing. I talk with the other applicants. Talk loudly. Talk to the other officials, who try to quiet me. I talk of how we, the born Stockholmers, are being dispossessed by the newcomers, the Scanians. Most of those listening are themselves not born in Stockholm but they applaud what I say with the eagerness of recent converts.

When the official comes back he begs my pardon. A slight slipup. Just a mistake. Of course I am on the list. I walk away to an old one-room flat that has become mine.

In a period of unemployment or economic crisis you would only need a thousand organized men who whipped up the emotions to get a pogrom against Scanians or redheads or what have you. All the nice people, the ordinary ones, would hunt them down the streets, string them up on lampposts or kick them to death.

Driving through the fog late one night, a hare rushes out in front of the car.

—Kill it! says E.

S steps on the gas. The car screeches around the bend and the hare jumps out into the fog. Disappears.

—Have often tried to kill a hare when driving, says S.

—They run fast, says K.

—The first time I shot a hare I was surprised to see how large a heart it had, says E. The lungs were large too. I was used to rabbits.

—Rabbits have hearts like writers, says S. Kill a writer and find a small heart.

We all laugh.

When I came to Oslo shortly after Liberation the streets were thronged with demonstrators believing that the world was to become better. We all went around cheering the politicians and generals. After one of the bigger demonstrations in the early autumn of 1945 my roommate brought a girl back to the apartment of the family with whom we lived. They had walked hand in hand in the demonstration. They didn't know each other. As far as I know they never met again. My roommate offered us home-grown tobacco. Reidar came. He had brought along some ship biscuit. An English soldier came. He had a bottle of brandy that he had liberated from the German stores he was guarding. He was a Cockney and a Red. We ate and drank and smoked and drank to Peace and World Socialism, and the People's future. We sang about the man who watered the Worker's beer. We sang a lot of songs. The future was so close. Just around the corner. As soon as the politicians and official leaders had settled their small differences. After a while the girl left and went home. Reidar went to his room. The Cockney stayed to empty the bottle, then he left and the party was over. Two months later I had nowhere to live. The people I was staying with had gotten their bombed-out relatives to move down to Oslo from North Norway. I had to move. One morning when I was walking along Karl Johan Street, frozen and numb after sleeping outdoors a couple of nights (on park benches), I met the girl. She was on the way to her job. We talked. She asked where I lived. I told her I didn't live anywhere. I pointed to the benches:

—The second bench to the left of the National Theatre is my home.

We laughed and she said that I could live at her place. I was to come up at seven o'clock that evening.

That whole day I sat—as I used to at that time—reading in the library. When it closed I walked the streets along the harbour. There was fog. In the evening I went to the girl's home. The block was solidly bourgeois. When I rang the bell the door was opened by a middle-aged woman who said:

—Ah! Jan Myrdal, I suppose?

Not giving me even a chance to answer she embraced me and kissed my right cheek. Then she took the black fibreboard box that contained all my earthly belongings (underwear, manuscripts, ship biscuit packed around an old Remington typewriter that for some reason was called "Streamliner") and carried it away. There were carpets, Afghan, and paintings, oil, and far off in a doorway a maid, starched white apron. An officer in uniform came up to me. He took me by the arm, above the elbow, and pushed me into a big room. He bade me welcome. Then he gave me a glass of brandy (French). Two elderly gentlemen asked to be introduced. Then the officer began asking me about my future.

They stood in a circle around me. My education? My plans for work? My income? Did I have any capital? Journalist? Poet? They looked at me with critical eyes. Scrutinized me. As they stared at me and talked towards me I felt a steeply rising horror in my bowels. But the thought of a soft bed to sleep in and—maybe, who knows? —even breakfast in the morning made me strain myself to sound friendly and presentable. I smiled as best I could. Felt the brandy in my veins; I was hungry, horribly hungry, and I thought the gentlemen had greasy lips as if they had just eaten. I hoped for a sandwich.

Now the girl stood in the doorway. She beckoned at me. I went up to her. Started talking. But she whispered:

—You know, they wondered why you should live here so I had to tell them we were engaged.

Then she left me. I was handed a new glass of brandy. Not without a certain hesitation though. The family continued questioning me. As the evening passed the atmosphere in the room became cold and unfriendly. There was a draught.

When everyone finally had gone to bed—the bed I was given was exquisite—I lay awake. When I was sure the house was sleeping I went to the girl's room. She was very pretty. I woke her up.

—But Jan, she said, you mustn't touch me. I love another. Then I went out into the hall, gathered all my clothes and took my black fibreboard box with typewriter, underwear, manuscripts and ship biscuit and sneaked out on the stairway. There I dressed. I shut the door softly behind me when I came out into the cold night. That was how I got engaged to marry the first time. I was one month past eighteen.

The impossibility of returning; the impossibility of even making understandable:

In the autumn of 1946 I was very much in love with a girl. For a short time we lived together. Then she left me for another man. As the circles in a country like Sweden are quite small I happened to meet her now and then throughout the years. We were always on good—albeit neutral—terms. Friendly you could say. But once, probably in 1953 or possibly in 1954, we met in a foreign town. It was very hot. We happened to stay at the same hotel. I was sitting on the rim of her bathtub while she was having a bath. She was sunburned and good-looking. Suddenly she said:

—You never really cared for me. That's why I left you. I never felt that you cared for me as a human being.

—But I did love you, I said. I really did. And two things I will never forget. One is your blond pubic hair as soft as silk and the other that once when I was sitting looking into the fire you said, "Don't look straight into the fire, Jan, you will destroy your beautiful eyes."

When I had said this she got very upset. She stood up, wrapped the bathrobe around herself and said that I had just confirmed what she always had felt. I was cynical and cold. I lacked the most elementary notions of human feelings. After that we were not even friends any more and now I have not seen her for many years. If I come into a room she leaves. What surprised me was that she in this way condemned some of the finest moments of my whole youth. It seemed impossible for her to accept that those two memories of her made up the whole sum of that love, both the sexuality and the tenderness.

In the thirties the kids fought each other in the Stockholm suburbs. They had then been fighting for a century. Formerly it had been students against apprentices. In the thirties it was the upper-middle-class houseowners' sons against the lower-middle-class houseowners' sons in a

middle-class suburb—Olovslund against Åkeshov. As far
as I know they still fight today. I read in my paper that
the police had raided the park where I grew up and found
submachine guns. The world is making progress.

Although I was but the son of an upper-middle-class
family that rented its house, I was nevertheless enlisted
in the Olovslund defence corps of houseowners' sons. The
older boys had stolen spiked helmets from an army surplus
store. They had also stolen old sabres. I was young, so
young as to be equipped only with a cudgel. We were all
members of the Civilian Defence and we had sawed-off
stretcher poles. When the war came we used to steal the
tear gas grenades that were used for gas training—but
that is another story.

We young ones had the honour of going first into
battle. Behind us were the older boys, those who studied
Latin and Greek. They had air guns and air pistols. They
used to climb up in the trees and shoot from there. We
had but slingshots in our hip pockets. In the highest trees
sat the leaders with spiked helmets and sabres over their
knees. They never took part in the fighting.

When we took prisoners from among the Åkeshovians
we were ordered to tie them to the fir trees in the park.
When we had done so the older boys came with their
air guns. They stood in a row and shot salt shots into
the thighs of the prisoners. The victims used to scream a
lot. (By the way, I might add that both the tormented
and the tormentors are long since grown up now. The
tormentors have passed the colleges and universities
and become high officials and executives. The tormented
exercise their universal suffrage and have become good
and well-tempered workers in the welfare state.) I myself was never shot with salt shots in the thigh. I only
had to hold my left hand over the touch hole of the
old powder pistol the leader used. I don't know why.

Maybe it was a good joke. I remember how we all laughed when the spike-helmeted leader pulled the trigger, and when I look at my left index finger today, twenty-five years later, it is still blue and scarred from the gunpowder impregnation.

But even I finally won fame and glory on this, the provincial, upper-middle-class houseowners' sons' field of honour. Being in the first line of charging Olovslunders I went too far among the enemy. I was surrounded. My cudgel was snatched away. My fate seemed sealed. But I found a rake and shouting the Olovslunder yell I swung the big rake around in a circle at face level while slowly retreating. The enemy was kept at a respectable distance. Then one of the Åkeshovians came running towards me with a long plank. He struck me over the head. The impact was paralyzing. I dropped the rake, my knees turned to jelly. But the plank had been broken against my head. I succeeded in remaining standing. The Olovslunders cheered with joy and renewed their attack. The Åkeshovians fled. Victory was ours. With blood streaming down over my shirt I staggered homewards. All around me the Olovslunders shouted:

—Stonehead Myrdal, Stonehead Myrdal.

Even the leaders were pleased with me.

Since then I have not felt any interest in national defence.

Words are tools. Thus I have respect for them. So I look at them with distrust; who wields them and with what purpose. If I had lacked this distrust I would have been sold long ago!

In the fall of 1956 I had just returned to Sweden. I visited S, an old friend of mine. He shared a flat on the south side in Stockholm with a businessman, U; a man of many ventures. We listen to the radio. We discuss Hungary and Suez.

In the middle of this conversation S suddenly says that it is too bad that he has so few bookshelves. He has lost them in his last divorce. Now his books are piled on the floor. U looks at him and says:

—But you can borrow mine. I have some shelves I don't need. They are in my boxroom in the garret of my old flat on Grevgatan. If you want to fetch them you may have them. But I have my keys in my country cottage, so you have to kick the door open. It is easy. And—by the way—don't let the caretaker see you; I owe him for cleaning the stairway.

I listen with half an ear to the conversation, the problem of bookshelves for S does not interest me in the least. I start talking about Hungary again. After half an hour I leave.

The next day S visits me in my flat on Skånegatan. He asks me to help him move the bookshelves. A secretary in the labour youth movement drives us to Grevgatan in the youth movement car. Together we all three carry the bookcases downstairs. It takes time. The bookshelves are placed in S's flat. Shortly thereafter U finds an heiress. Marries her, moves from the flat he shared with S and takes the bookshelves along. He leaves one for S. S and I are not invited to the wedding. U believes that we will make a bad impression on the new family. He is to become vice-president of one of the family companies. S feels hurt. I don't care. I never liked U, just talked to him because S was an old friend.

A month later I meet the photographer O at an exhibition. He cuts me dead. He makes a detour around me. I get irritated, I ask him:

—What the hell is the matter with you? Are you going blind?

—A joke is a joke, he answers. But to break into my
attic and steal my bookshelves is no joke. It is theft and
burglary. I didn't go to the police, but I don't have to see
you any more either.
I explained.

But if U by manipulating words succeeded in making
me and the law-abiding S and the young politician (who
would have become a national disgrace to the Labour
party if he had been caught) commit burglary, how much
easier is it not for the great interests to manipulate prejudices and idiosyncrasies, misinformation, agony, ideals
and religions to get people to fool themselves?

K spoke about his childhood.
—My father had a farm near Enköping, north of Lake
Mälar. He was well liked. He used to give a party after
Christmas every year. I could hear the men talking and
singing until I fell asleep. In the morning my schoolmates
came with wheelbarrows. Then we loaded their fathers
on the wheelbarrows. You know, it was such fun. The snow
was gleamingly white on all the fields, the forests were
green and the birches covered with hoarfrost. A long procession of boys in red woollen caps were pushing black
wheelbarrows through this landscape. The fathers were all
snoringly drunk, their legs dangled, and we all used to
sing. My father was such a popular man. Winters are different now. They just rain.

Physical activity has always appealed to me. I have
worked on a trapeze, studied yoga, walked in the mountains, marched through Sweden and the greater part of
Europe with all my belongings in a rucksack. I have never
had any major difficulties. I was born with a strong phy-
sique. I have always been robust and supple without
having to care about physical training. During certain

periods, though, I have even been well trained. During
the years and the ramblings I have hurt, crushed, smashed,
broken and battered different parts of my body; toes,
fingers, ears and nose have been frostbitten (not so badly,
though, that they were totally lost). Until I got run over
by a police car last year I was in good shape.

But the merry cry:

—Now, let's all eighteen go and take a bath!

I have always found repulsive. And I have never had any
understanding for organized (by others) forms of physical
exercise. My repugnance to collective sweating at the order
of some tooth-grinning leader has of course brought me
into several conflicts.

I went to Lincoln High School in New York. It was a
progressive school at that time, just before the Second
World War. You know, development of personality and
all that. Bringing out the inherent gifts of the pupil. The
school had a rather good library and a gloomy baseball
field. (Some slum houses had been torn down and we
were supposed to play on the site.)

I preferred to sit in the library. After a month or two the
teachers carefully tried to steer my personality in the direction of baseball. I pointed out that this did not fit in with
the ideals the school had proclaimed. Free development of
personality.

At this stage I was sent to the school psychologist. It
was a woman. She had an aura of understanding. She
seemed so understanding that I immediately became suspicious. She tested me and found that I lacked group-
mindedness. With understanding she wanted to correct
this. I protested. I demanded my right freely to sit in the
library reading. She meant that the school had the task
of helping me to develop freely as a gardener helps a rose.
It seemed that American roses needed group-mindedness
and baseball. I said that possibly the school might under-

stand that there were personalities that wanted to freely develop in the direction of libraries. It might even be possible for me to organize such a group in the school if I were left in peace. Then there would be two groups of group-minded pupils. One group in the baseball field and one group in the library. She pointed out that the very fact that I was arguing was symptomatic of the deep psychological disturbance that made my free development into a happy and group-minded American impossible. I said that I believed I could bear my lack of group-mindedness. Yes; I even looked forward to a long life without this —for her undoubtedly necessary—quality. That I, both then and in the future, might become part of a collective, but a collective I would choose myself.

For two years teachers and psychologists with understanding and tenderness fought to drive me out of the library. I emerged victorious because I was stubborn. But it was very unpleasant. Sometimes even painful. After all, I was but twelve years old, and they were a collective of tender and group-minded grownups. Then I decided that my children would never have to go to a school that with tenderness tried to help them develop their personality freely—like a rose.

When I came home to Sweden during the war I was put in the Bromma Secondary School. One of the first lessons in this new school was to be physical training. I went to the gym at the appointed time and said:

—They told me I was to begin here.

But I had no more than said this and taken two steps into the hall when the teacher (he was a doctor of physical education) got blue in the face, his eyes turned red, he stared at me and shouted:

—You there! You get out! I don't ever want to see you here!

At that I left. And I never came back. For the three
years I went to the Bromma Secondary School (until I got
expelled), I sat in the library (which was quite good)
when the others went to do physical training. Nobody
tried to adjust me.

Even if the result was not unpleasant, still the reception
had surprised me. As far as I knew the man had never seen
me before. Only much later did I understand what had
happened.

This doctor of the science of physical education had a
deep passion for the floor of his gym. The gleaming var-
nish was soft as the maidenhood of a young girl (a theoretical girl of course). And then I had entered: fat,
gold-rimmed glasses, crew-cut hair, a striped sweater
(yellow and brown), shorts and hobnailed boots. And if
my whole appearance was a gum-chewing blasphemy, my
boots were a sin against that immaculate conception.

From this I draw the conclusion that it might be easier
to freely develop one's personality in an old-fashioned
school among mad teachers without either understanding
or tenderness.

In June 1945 I was cub reporter on the *Arbetar-Tid-
ningen* in Gothenburg. As I was the youngest on the editorial staff I was sent to cover the Women's Auxiliary Corps
Summer Festival. It was held at the Gothenburg Gardens
in the middle of the town.

The main attraction was to be a table-decorating com-
petition for the starving children of Europe. The most
well-known hostesses of Gothenburg were to lay tables
(candles, silver, wine glasses) on a stage in front of the
audience. My throat got dry. I was seventeen. It was June
1945. (The proceeds were to go to the fund for starving
children.) I went back to the newspaper office and wrote

an article reeking of sulphur that expressed all my indignation. Then I looked at what I had written. Tore it up.

Wrote another article instead, a funny one. Quoted the names of these gentle ladies. The aesthetic tables for good dinner parties. The starving children of Europe. Cold writing with all the names would be effective, I thought. The readers would laugh, understand and despise. I trusted the readers. And the readers did laugh. They shared my indignation.

But the next day the people in the advertising department called up. They demanded my head. All these leading ladies of the Women's Auxiliary Corps were married to the leading advertisers. They had now declared an economic boycott. One day later the paper apologized in an editorial: "An Indiscretion."

Then I realized that even in the most left-wing newspapers the liberty is the liberty to go within the bounds the market sets.

If you write satire, write it against charwomen, prostitutes, narcotics addicts and lower-middle-class suburban women. But never, never, never write about the wives of generals, leading executives, consuls general and colonels.

That was the end of my career on that paper.

The last summer that was a childhood summer of mine was the warm summer of 1941. My paternal aunt and her husband were taking care of me then. They had rented a summer house on an island in Lake Mälar. The island was large; the Black Sealand was its name.

My uncle was in the army, of course. He said they were building fortifications along the eastern coast. He said the men distrusted the officers. All the weapons had been sent last year to Finland. Outside of Kalmar the company had started singing the "Internationale." The men had been

sent to work camps in the northern forests. I listened to
all this. Sat reading in the afternoons. Now and then there
was a thunderstorm. Lightning hit the house. Nobody was
hurt. It was a fireball. It rolled in through the wall socket.
Rolled swishing along the ceiling and burst through the
window. Afterwards it smelled. My aunt cried.

On June 15 my uncle said:

—The Russians are saying that the friendship between
Russia and Germany is solid. That means that war is imminent.

The day I heard about the German attack it was raining.
I sat in the dining room with my school atlas. I drew battle
maps.

Later that summer I bicycled up to Dalecarlia. It was
no use going by train. The trains were all full. And they
were always delayed. We were transporting German
troops to the front, I was told.

I started to work on a farm. The family were distant
relatives. At the end of August I fell down from the hay-
loft and struck my head against the floor. Was in bed for
some time. Then school started. Our German teacher said
that a new order had begun for Europe.

In February 1952 I was going to London to visit my then
mother-in-law. I had stayed in Strasbourg for a couple of
days. Visited a friend of mine who had been a jazz fan
and now worked for the Council of Europe. He had a
nice house and read science fiction. (Later he became a
bank director, one of the leading financiers of Sweden. I
have not seen him for many years now.) I hitchhiked.
It rained. The wind blew cold over northern France and I
composed a poem. (Bad.) Was tired.

Got aboard the ferry at Dunkirk just as it was about to
leave. I was the only passenger. The weather was bad on
the crossing but when we arrived at Dover in the morning

the sun was shining. A cold sun. I went ashore and the immigration officer took my passport. He slowly turned the leaves over, said:

—What is the purpose of your visit?

—Visit my mother-in-law.

—What is her name?

I told him. He looked at me and said:

—She can't be your mother-in-law. That's an Indian name.

—She is married to a Bengali, I said.

—Do you expect me to believe that? he said.

—Call London and check, I said.

—I am the one to decide what is to be done, not you. When was the last time you met this mother-in-law?

—I have never met her, I said. She was in London when I married her daughter.

—Give me straight answers. Where is your wife? he said.

—She is in Geneva, I said.

—It doesn't say in your passport that you are married, he said.

—We don't do that in Sweden, I said.

—Do you expect me to believe that? he said.

—That is easy to check, I said.

—Don't use that tone to me, he said. You better be polite. Why have you deserted your wife?

—She goes to the Beaux-Arts in Geneva and it is the middle of the term, I said.

—So you have deserted her, he said and made notes in his little black book.

—I want to speak to the superior officer, I said. This is ridiculous.

—I am the superior officer, he said. Why have you crossed the border between Switzerland and France illegally?

—I have never crossed any borders illegally, I said.

—The number of departures from Switzerland is not in accordance with the number of entries into France and the departures from France do not coincide with the entries into Switzerland, and the dates of the stamps are all wrong, he said.

—Usually they don't stamp the passports at all when you cross from Geneva to Ferney-Voltaire, I said.

—Do you expect me to believe that? he said and made further notes in his little black book.

—This is absolutely ridiculous, I said. Why don't you call London and check what I am telling you?

—That is not for you to decide, he said. Why do you speak English? You have never been in Great Britain.

—I grew up in the United States, I said.

—You are lying, he said. You don't have an American accent.

—What do you know about America? I said. Have you been there?

—I have warned you against using that tone, he said. I am the one who puts the questions.

—This is madness, I said. Please let me talk to somebody.

—Why have you absconded from America? he said.

—But, I have never run away from anything, I said.

—So that means that you were deported from America, he said. Nobody leaves America.

—But this is indecent, I said. Please, please check what I am saying.

—You are un-American, are you not? he said.

—Telephone London, I said.

He wrote in his little black book. A thin man in a grey trench coat, his teeth were ratlike and yellow.

—How long have you been a Kominform courier? he said.

—You are stark, raving mad, I said.

—Your behaviour gives you away, he said. They always protest. You have been to Yugoslavia. See here; it is in your passport: "Viza Br. V 3/48 ulazno-izlazna" January 10, 1948.

—Do you ever read the newspapers? I said. Happen to know about a man named Tito?

—Don't be evasive, he said. East is East.

—I demand to see a sensible person, I said.

—Just a moment, he said.

He left the room. He took my passport along and I stood at the desk, waiting. When he came back he brought along three policemen. They took me away. First they searched my luggage. They rolled out my sleeping bag and felt it inch by inch. They did not roll it back. Then they searched my pockets. In my wallet they found a letter from *Clarté*: "Why not try to take some subscriptions for the magazine in Geneva? There must be sensible persons even there. Greetings. John."

—*Clarté*, he said. That sounds subversive.

Then they undressed me. They had to use a certain amount of force. The letter from *Clarté* he put in an envelope and stuck the envelope in his little black book. When I was naked a man in a white apron entered. He was called doctor. He pulled on india-rubber gloves and ran his fingers up my rectum.

—Nothing there, he said to the immigration officer. Then he left.

—You may dress now, a policeman said.

They told me to put my luggage in order. Then I was brought back to the hall.

—I am going to deport you, the immigration officer said. You are an undesirable alien.

He carefully put a stamp in my passport on page 22.

Then he looked at it and stamped first a vertical and then a horizontal bar over it. "Immigration officer (20) 16 Feb 1952 Dover."

—There, he said.

—I demand to call my embassy, I said.

—You have full right to speak with your embassy, he said. In Britain we follow international law.

I went to the telephone but he put up his hand, stopped me and said:

—This is an official telephone. You can't use that. You have to use the public telephone.

—Good, I said, where is it?

—There, he said, over there. But you have to pay in British currency. And you don't have any. You have only got traveller's cheques.

—I will change them, I said.

—Sorry, he said. That can only be done at Cook's and before the Cook's people come I will have you put aboard the ship. Sorry.

That was the first time he smiled.

—You are not a British subject, he said.

Then I was taken away by two policemen. I was kept locked up in a cell. The two policemen were sitting beside me all the time.

—You really would like to make a phone call, wouldn't you? said one.

—You damn fucking foreigner, said the other.

When they got me aboard the steward wanted me to pay for my deportation. I refused. I told him they would get their fare in hell.

—Why do we British have to take care of all these foreigners? the steward said. Dover has to send them back every day and they won't even pay.

When I came back to France I was stamped in by the same man who had stamped me out the night before.

—These Englishmen, he said. They are mad. But we are a civilized country. In France you are always welcome, monsieur.

Later I spoke to a British diplomatic representative in Geneva. It was an unfortunate accident, he said. I asked him to get me a written apology.

—I am sorry, he said, we never give a foreigner an official apology. It is against our policy.

—Very well, I said. Until I get a written apology I will never return to Britain.

Speaking about national traits:
I grew up listening to talk of kinship and ancestors. The world seemed filled with cousins. (English is a poor language in which to describe this. Not even a word for third-degree cousins; no distinction between paternal and maternal lines.) I mean filled. Whether in the United States or Sweden there were always cousins (at least in fourth or fifth degree) around somewhere. Of course one didn't have to like them—but one could always appeal to kinship. (You can always stay overnight with a cousin.)

When I learned to read I could follow my ancestors in the family register. I was not abnormally interested. But I could not help wondering how come my father's-mother's-mother's-mother's-mother's-mother's-father's-father Göran Hansson in Moren had got the name "the Impudent." Of course, they had to call him something to distinguish him from my father's-mother's-mother's-mother's-father's-mother's-father's-mother's-father who was also named Göran Hansson and lived in Moren but who was fourteen years younger (being born 1708). But why just "the Impudent"? And I felt suspicious about the birth of my father's-father's-mother's-mother's-mother Brita Persdotter because she was born half a year after the death of her father Trost Per Ersson in March 1777. (But

I was careful not to ask anybody. I still feel guilty thinking about it. After all, it was said about Trost Per Ersson that he was "honest" and about his wife Malin Danielsdotter that she was "honest and God-fearing.")

There has been peace in Sweden since the Napoleonic wars but before that there were great wars. The wars of Charles XII are the best known to non-Swedes. It is also a statistical fact that a large part of the Swedish male population (as we had a kind of national service) died in those wars. But it was a standing family joke that we had never lost an ancestor in any war. Like all jokes it was not quite correct. My father's-mother's-mother's-mother's-father's-father's-mother's-father's-father the soldier number 90 Daniel Hvigg fought in Finland and disappeared in Pomerania. He probably was killed (if he did not manage to desert). And my father's-father's-father's-father's-father's-mother's-father Peder Hansson disappeared in 1704 from Säter and it was said that he might have run off to war.

Some miles to the southwest of where I am writing this died my mother's-father's-father's-father's-father Jan Jansson. He was known as "the juror." The villagers had elected him as one of the twelve lay judges of the Thing in Härad county. He was a respected man.

I have my name from them, Jan from the maternal line and Myrdal from the paternal (as a child I used to think about the name; signed an essay at school: "Yahweh-has-been-gracious Swampy-riverside"; the teacher said I was indecent, but I protested and said that I had the right to correctly translate my own name).

All over Sweden you will find them in the new suburbs; white-collar workers sitting and collecting their ancestors to the fourteenth degree. Filling notebooks with the names of petty peasants in thousands. And they all sound the same, Jan Jansson, Peder Hansson, Hans Pedersson, Per Ersson. All except the ones who became soldiers and were given "real" names by their officers: Stolt = proud, Stark = strong (like the slaves in the United States).

And I hear foreigners, coming to see the suburbs, talking of "Modern Sweden." The foreigners just don't know that if they scrape the surface of these suburbs they will find a nation of petty peasants.

—During Partition, said Ram Kishan, I went to school in Rawalpindi. When the Muslims began to slit the throats of the Hindus and the Hindus started slaughtering the Muslims and I heard what was happening everywhere I decided to start homeward. I was young at that time and could be taken for a Muslim, so nobody suspected me. When I got nearer to my home village I only walked at night. I did not want to be seen by any Muslim who knew me. When I arrived at our village on the Jhelum it seemed deserted. Many houses were in ruins. But I entered the village anyway. When I came to our house I saw that my maternal uncle's head had been hung up in the doorway. I understood that there had been real trouble there. In the yard lay my paternal grandmother and two of my sisters. I left and went across the fields trying to let nobody see me. Two days later when I was walking eastwards a man came. He saw me. He didn't know who I was. He said:

—Why are you walking eastwards?

—I want to kill Hindus, I said.

—Then we can keep each other company, he said.

Thus we walked for several days towards the border. Everywhere there was great unrest and many dead. Later I managed to slip away and was alone once more. The man had thought I was a Muslim. He had trusted me. I managed to cross the border and now I live here. But Rawalpindi was such a beautiful town.

That is what I remember from Liberation.

. . .

One evening in the spring of 1951 I went around in the
Annedal district of Gothenburg collecting names for an
appeal for a peace treaty between the Great Powers. I
was on the first floor and rang the bell. The house was
built around 1910. A man opened the door. He took the
appeal, said:

—Of course I will sign.

When he got it in his hands he tore it up in small
pieces. Ten signatures were written on that appeal, and
the man said:

—I am a democratic citizen. I believe in freedom. I
believe in the Rights of Man. You damn traitor.

Then he slammed the door shut. Thus these ten signatures were never accounted for.

In February 1957 we had been drinking in Málaga. We
had been drinking the whole way. From the upper-class
bars down to the hole in the wall near the harbour where
the brandy was half a peseta per glass. In one place, the
bar of the Alegría restaurant, a couple of whores had
tried to pick us up. But I had said to my friend:

—If we have never paid for it before, why should we
start paying now?

My friend agreed. After all a man who has to pay in
order to be liked loses both his morals and his self-respect.
But we felt sorry for the girls. They had their jobs to
tend to. We drank with them and paid for their drinks.
Soon they were out of the picture. Once more the bars,
the quays, the hole in the wall. Suddenly we were back
at our hotel. We lived on the third floor. There was an
open courtyard in the middle of the house. The balustrade
was low and my friend dived over it. That was when
we had reached the second floor. I managed to grab his
left leg and he crawled back and said:

—You have always been a good friend.

I didn't feel quite well when I came to my room. My friend had the room next to mine. He bellowed. Regularly as a foghorn he bellowed through the night. He used to do so when he was blind drunk and sick. His bellowing echoed through the hotel.

I wake up in the morning with the sun shining on my eyeballs and the shakes hit my stomach; greater anguish squeezes my heart; throat dry and red sun. There is knocking at my door. I have spewed all over the floor. More knocking. But the floor is a stone one and easy to clean. I throw cold water on my neck. It trickles down my spine. I dip my face in cold water. I start to clean the floor. The whole time the knocking continues. I use the hotel towel to clean up. The room becomes quite tidy. It just knocks and knocks. I wrap the dirty towel in a newspaper. In fact it is a fascist sheet named *Ideal,* published in Granada. I nearly laugh. I stiffen myself, put a nice smile on my face, try to clear my eyes, and open the door. There stands the chambermaid. She is old. I greet her courteously and fetch my friend. He is already awake and we walk along. But before we have reached the staircase we see the chambermaid looking after us, she speaks to somebody and I start running with my head hidden between my shoulders. I have the parcel under my arm. When we reach safety on the street I want to leave the parcel, but my friend says:

—Somebody might find it and see that it is the hotel towel.

We run towards the harbour. The guard stops us but we pass. We are to hide the towel. Everywhere people stare at us. They come out from every corner and point accusing fingers at us. We walk along the stone quays, try to hide behind the sheds. Now the guards begin to gather and follow us. We sweat. We run fast. They chase

us. Eyes stare, fingers point. The ship far out. All the
time sun and I sweat and the heart only anguish.

We are far from the harbour now. Trees. I hide the
parcel under a park bench. But a policeman walks towards us and we fetch the parcel again.

—You know, says my friend, they will recognize the
name of the hotel.

We sit on a bench further away. He cuts the towel in
small pieces with his moustache scissors. (He bought
them in Hong Kong, they are beautiful, have yellow inlay
and a case of pigskin. He always carries them in his breast
pocket.) Now we walk along the esplanade. Try to look
strolling. Now and then we bend down and hide a piece
of the towel. Two policemen start to follow us. They
walk behind us. Coming closer. We run. Another hour
has passed. We have hidden the last piece. Only the
small piece with the hotel name remains. We try to burn
it, but my lighter runs out of fuel. We throw the lighter
away. The sun shines. Around us is a ring of people,
all staring. They don't do anything. Just stare. I hold the
piece of cloth with the embroidered name between my
right thumb and forefinger. Looking at it I see that it is
charred at the edges. Under my arm I hold the newspaper. *Ideal.* Now we are once more running towards the
harbour. We find a string and I wrap the newspaper
around a stone. Make a parcel out of it with the string.
I have forgotten the piece of cloth. It is not in the parcel.
My friend stands holding it in his hand. I fasten the piece
of cloth outside the parcel. A man stands smoking beside
us. He looks. We walk further out on the pier. There we
throw the parcel in the sea. It sinks but the piece of
cloth with name floats up. It stares reproachingly at me.
Beside it a contraceptive. We walk towards the town
again. Now many people are following us but we try to

look as if we don't see them. My friend makes out that he is telling a good joke and I try to laugh in a well-mannered way. My friend says that he has the small shakes. We have a brandy. When we feel better we take two more. When we come back to the hotel they have already packed our luggage. It stands in the lobby. They give me my bill. The towel is the last item on the bill. We pay. Nobody says anything. Then a man comes towards me and wishes me a good journey. He says I am welcome back. We go down towards the harbour. I see the ship.

In 1958 I went to a party given by a Swedish arms dealer in Delhi. A young maharajah in white dinner jacket with small pink hands and well-kept nails says:

—What this country needs is discipline. A strong hand at the helm is needed. The people here in India have never understood the need of discipline. That is why our history has been what it has been. And now it just goes from bad to worse. The British at least tried to keep the mob in order. But the way things are now I don't know how it will end. When I was out hunting the day before yesterday, for instance, I had parked my jeep where the road ended. When I came back some peasants were sitting in the jeep. They fingered everything. They are just like children, you know. I told them to get out of my car. But one of them answered back. He said, "The car is standing on my land." Then I took my gun and pointed it at his chest and said, "Get out!" But he still tried to answer and said, "This is a free country now." Then I said, "I will count to three and then I will shoot you." He still remained sitting. Then I started to count: "One, two . . . " Then they both ran. They jumped out of the car and just ran like rabbits. I sent a shot over

their heads to teach them. One of them was so afraid
that he fell flat on his stomach in the mud. Such a thing
would never have happened in the old days. There must
be discipline or our country will perish. And honestly,
I must say that if our government doesn't have the guts
to clean up this country, then I know who will. We,
the educated classes, will never let India down.

When I was young I had a friend who was—or at
least said he was—an epileptic. He also was Herule,
Kretschmerian athlete, drug addict and artist. The last,
being an artist, was the operative. Everything else was
but explanations for his—to us at that time undoubted—
genius. One evening in October 1947 he and I are sitting
in the restaurant of Wexjö City Hotel. We drink gin
and tonic. Then he leans over the table, looks me gravely
in the eyes and says:

—You know, Jan, I believe that you too are an epileptic.
Or at least that you suffer from petit mal.

—You really mean that? I say.

—Sure, he says. Sure. Skål!

I still remember the immense pride I felt when I—
on false papers though—was promoted to the class of
genius.

When I was seven I was very much in love with a girl
named Anne who was my classmate. Not only I but my
friend Gabriel too was in love with her. Seven years
later, in 1941, when I was fourteen and had come back
from the United States and begun to think of myself as a
man, I was sitting talking with Gabriel one Sunday afternoon. We spoke about Anne and decided to visit her.

We took the streetcar to where she lived, went upstairs and rang the bell. A fair girl with red sleep in her
eyes opened the door. She still had long hair. Tousled.
She looked at us. After a moment she said:

—You'll have to excuse me. I am tired. I was at a dance yesterday. But you have grown, I can see. Long trousers and hats!

I was seventeen. It was late fall 1944. I worked as a cub reporter for *Värmlands Folkblad.* I earned twenty-five crowns a week. That is five dollars. Not very much. Was not very much even then. But I rented a room with direct entrance from the street. I worked the night shift. I wrote. And often—strange to say—the written was printed. I had borrowed a liquor ration book (we had liquor permits in Sweden from the First World War until 1957). I had a girl who visited me in my room a couple of times a week. (She didn't want to be seen with me in town, she said.) And every morning when I woke up I drank a toothbrush glass full of brown, sticky, Swedish, wartime ersatz cacao liqueur. In short, resolutely, I was stepping out into the free and happy life of the grownups.

The summer was of my earliest childhood. The sky was blue and white clouds hung over the fir forest. The grass was green and the humming of bees. Then I saw my first hedgehog. It came towards me over the gravel walk. The roses burned red. I rushed towards it and said:
—Come! You little animal.
Then I patted it lovingly. I still have a strong memory of how my hands were dipped in a bowl filled with hydrogen peroxide. It boiled and hissed in the wounds and I screamed. How I screamed!

A night in July 1946 I borrow a canoe and paddle across the bay. The night is dark and cloudy and there is a hard wind blowing in from the Åland Sea. I am to see a blond girl.

In winter half a year later I am in love with a girl. She has black hair and laughs. She is intellectual and artistic and I exert myself to be able to give her smoked eel and wine and I love her much.

In the summer of 1950 I see Gustaf in Kristianstad. First we go to his church, he plays a composition of his on the organ, then he plays jazz. The echoes roll in the empty seventeenth-century church of the Holy Trinity. Then we go to the Masonic Lodge hotel. He takes in the large smorgasbord. We talk about life and art. Together with an old journalist from *Kristianstad-Läns-Demokraten* (The Kristianstad County Democrat) we go home to Gustaf's and continue drinking. The journalist buys an article off me for ten crowns. He did sometimes. The comptroller-manager of the paper refused to let him pay more. In the morning Gustaf says that we must begin a new life. We drink yoghurt and eat raw carrots and talk of life and art.

In August 1952 I am drifting down from North Norway. Reach Oslo. I stay with Alex and Nic. Alex slaps my knee. We talk of how we shared an apartment for some weeks in November 1945. Nic pours the drinks and later on she talks of Erling Winsnes who was a genius and died in 1935. (I didn't read him until 1957.) She speaks about my unpublished books.

The blond girl is dead. She died of poliomyelitis. The dark girl is dead. She died in a car crash. Gustaf is dead. He died of cancer. The journalist is dead. The *Kristianstad-Läns-Demokraten* has been closed down. Alex drowned in a mountain lake. Nic is dead. In 1960, when I return to Sweden, I suddenly find that a great part of my youth is already gone. There is nothing left and these memories I share with nobody.

.   .   .

To be fifteen was hell. But to become sixteen was still worse. I may have been thinking with my great brain —I must have as I was ploughing my way through all the classics, through the contemporary Swedish writers, through political economy, history, philosophy—but I acted with my medulla oblongata. Or my glands. Or rather, I tried to act, but with little success. Some necking in the parks. That was all. I was sixteen and it was a horror to live in a world so prudish and delicate. (A double horror as every time my big brain functioned I knew how murderous this prudish world was.)

But—some days after my seventeenth birthday I lay with my first woman. And I still remember it. It was just as dizzyingly liberating as I had dreamt. And it was so wonderful and it was so beautiful and when I walked home in the early morning the sun was burning red in the bark of the pines and the water under the bridge was a bright mirror. I remember looking out over the sleeping city and shouting from high up on the concrete bridge:

—Life is happiness.

But . . . I had told the girl that I was eighteen and just about to become nineteen. (Seventeen was such a ridiculous age, I felt. And of course I had not told her she was my first either.) The next night she looked at me with big eyes and said:

—Jan darling, I never want to let you go. We could petition the king and get a dispensation for marriage and then we could be together for always.

Then everything collapsed around me. The kisses tasted of ashes. I tore myself loose, grabbed my pants and rushed in horror from her place. I ran and ran and ran through the night and it drizzled.

In Teheran, in 1958, it struck me that cars belonging to generals, millionaires and the well-connected drove through red lights. Gradually I found that driving through red lights was a social privilege. (The Americans working there had the national privilege of being airlifted out of the country by their embassy if they had happened to kill somebody while driving.)

The social privilege of driving through red lights seemed to me akin to the remaining privilege of the Swedish nobility: the right of being executed by sword in case of high treason during war.

In the spring of 1945 I come to Gothenburg just after the end of the war in Europe. Erik has got a flat. He is going to get married. It is a basement flat. There are two beds. One blanket and one mattress. Hasse, who has been working on a ship outside the blockade during the war, comes to Gothenburg. He and I move to Erik's place. It is damp. The wallpaper has mildewed to a velvety texture. We draw lots about the beds. I get one of the beds for myself. Erik and Hasse share the other. Since they are two they get the mattress. I cover the springs with old newspapers. But as they are two they can keep each other warm, and I get the blanket and they share Hasse's overcoat. In the mornings we have milk with bread and butter and Hasse has got some real coffee, which we share.

In Ceylon I talk to a nice European tea planter:
—How many are there in this district? I ask.
—We are only four families, he says.
—That's not much, I say.
—And, of course, twenty-five thousand Tamils, he says.

In October 1933 we live on the Stockholm waterfront. I am sitting at the window and look out over the harbour. A tug is pulling barges along the canal. The sky is grey. Mary says:

—Maybe they go to the warm South.

—Sure, I say. If they go far enough they then have to continue to the warm North.

—Don't be stupid, she says.

After that I repeated this test with many grownups and found that most of them had never realized that the earth is round.

As a child I spent long periods with my paternal grandparents. My parents were often abroad and my grandmother was to take care of me. She was a religious believer. This gave me problems of conscience. Because whenever I discussed religion with her she did not change her beliefs even though my arguments were good; she only began to worry and suffer from insomnia. At the same time it was difficult for me to accept a view of life that was so strange and so different from everything I had met from my own parents, from my playmates, from my maternal grandfather and in nursery school.

I liked the old woman, though, and I felt sad to hear her cry. So I solved the problem by making her happy and reading a prayer at night with a loud voice. Under my breath I then added, "Of course I know this is not so. There are no gods. There is no life after death. I know all religion is superstition." In this way I kept on every night during the times she took care of me until I became eleven years old. Then I went with my parents to the USA. When I came home and once more met my paternal grandmother and she once more took care of the family —as my parents stayed in America during the war— there was no need for me to be hypocritical any longer. Partly because I was so old that she was no longer present when I went to bed and partly because my grandfather being dead and my father in America, I was the oldest male in the family.

. . .

On the plains, in the deserts, the sun is a white ball of
fire in a sky grey with heat. The wind sweeps dry over
the cracked earth, there is no shadow and no hiding place
from the light, the heat, the drought. The hours pass and
in the hot wind I feel my brain shrivel up, the eyes want
to escape from the burned-out yellow, the sunshine, but
there is nowhere to go and the grey sky is a lump of fear
inside my chest. And the days become weeks and always
the same sun and the same hot afternoon when the heat
sucks the black cliffs, and dread of the nauseating ap-
proach of heatstroke, and the skin dry. The land without
shadows, the sky is without mercy and I listen to the motor
and feel the tires slipping in the sand.

Of course the greatest physical pleasure that I—like
all sexually reproducing animals—have experienced or
can experience is that of coitus. It is also impossible to describe. There are no words to describe experiences during
which no words can be formulated. Language is a tool.

I spent the summer of 1949 in a small cottage in South
Sweden trying to write a coitus. I don't mean a technical
description—that is easy; neither do I mean pornography.
(Though at certain times in certain cultures almost anything can be branded as indecent. Even piano legs.)
That was the time I tried to go through the Flaubertian
training. Describing trees. But however much I sweated
over my typewriter that summer and whatever formal
innovations and techniques I tried, I found it impossible.
Pornography I could write, of course. But that is simple.
There you use the culturally determined responses to
words in order to heighten tension. (I see no greater reason
for it though—socially it has nearly always served reactionary purposes—but that is another matter.)

In September I gave up the experiment. It was physiologically impossible. In the foreplay one still experiences oneself as an individual. That is possible to describe. But then, when the tensions increase and one is carried forward on a rising wave of instinct, all the reactions become different. The eyes react to light, breathing becomes fast, and as these physiological changes continue the consciousness too changes tone. The words disintegrate, the sense of time is shifted and after that the release, the small death. Only thereafter back to a normal level, describable. The sleepiness after coitus is describable. But the sexual experience is no pleasure. Pleasure is a false word. It is pleasure to eat when you are hungry and drink when you are thirsty, to scratch when it itches and stretch when you wake up in the morning. But a coitus is no pleasure. It is of a different quality. It can be mentioned, it can be measured, but it cannot be described or compared.

On this I think when I have come in from the desert to the small town. I am squatting naked in a dark room and now Gun pours a ladle of cold water over me. The jet of water hits my skin just between the shoulder blades. The sensation cuts through my body, my heart beats faster, my breathing becomes deep, my head falls forward, and all the time cold water covers my body, and suddenly I know that this bath can only be interpreted in sexual terms. It is not identical, but the dizzying experience is of the same kind. The cold water in the dark room over the tormented, parched, sun-racked body. And ever more water, and more and more. Finally falling asleep with wet clothes around the body, clothes gradually drying in the heat and in drying cooling the body.

So it can be compared. And as the sexual instinct makes people willingly undergo long and unhappy and often mentally and morally degrading marriages only for the oceanic sensation of communion twice a week, so I notice that my body is craving for the deserts, the heat, the merciless sun and the anxious listening to the motor, only to be able to experience the annihilation and indescribable bliss of the water.

In February 1956 when I lived at the Hotel Orfila in Paris (writing a book about teenage revolt in Sweden and greeting the shadow of Strindberg with calvados) and my unborn daughter was still but an eight-month-old fetus, I observed that every time I slammed two books together just above the mother's abdomen the fetus started to kick.

The first time I observed it I thought it was just a coincidence. But after a series of experiments I found that there was a real cause-and-effect relationship between the slamming and the kicking. It was not just coincidental.

My thought then was that the mother was responding and that the fetus only reacted as a consequence of her reaction. The mother might by reflex action contract her muscles at the slamming and the fetus might react against this contraction. Alternatively one might conceive of a sudden intensification of the mother's heart activity or other physiological reactions that released the kickings from the fetus. After a series of control experiments I could rule out both these possibilities. Subjecting the mother to minor shocks and sudden sounds other than slamming, it became quite evident that the fetus's movements after my slamming the books together was a specific reaction to a certain sound, or rather, a certain kind of vibration.

Then I investigated whether I, by slamming the books in different rhythm-patterns, could get the fetus to react in a more complicated "dancelike" way. The fetus, however, soon proved unable to distinguish between different rhythms. It seemed able to distinguish only between slamming noise and non-slamming noise. But the reaction time between noise and kick grew shorter and shorter. If this occurred because the fetus had "trained" its reflexes or because of its physiological development, I don't know. (An answer to that would demand a long series of experiments in which the normal reaction time for "untrained" fetuses at different stages of development could be established and then compared with the reaction time of fetuses at the same stage of development but with a longer period of "training.") For natural reasons my experiments were interrupted after a couple of weeks. (Looking on when the girl was born I felt sure—as I have done every time I have seen a birth—that the tremendous physiological shock of being pressed forward into this cold life of ours is the basis of the instinctive fear of death all of us—men and other animals—suffer from.)

Personally I am inclined to consider intelligence as mainly being an environmental effect. A postnatal environment that during the first months gives the newborn child possibilities to develop its reflexes, its muscular coordination and its paths of association in almost continuous contact with human skin and warm—but not hysterically damp—human hands, where the newborn child never experiences the sensation of losing its support (having to "get a grip") and where the rhythm of life is a self-adjustment, is, as far as I can understand, the best basis for the development of an all-round intellectual and physical intelligence.

This fast-reacting fetus did actually—in an environment similar to the above-mentioned—develop into a strong and clearly overintelligent girl. (As a baby she showed unusually little need of sleep; later on the traits of stubbornness, utter self-reliance and lack of what people call "contact" proved to be predominant in her character and gave her difficulties. But I doubt if there is any connection. The "character" seems rather an adaptation to the ideal stereotype of the elders in the kinship system.)

But—if a series of experiments would show that children who were obviously overintelligent at the age of seven had also been faster-reacting fetuses at the age of eight prenatal months than those children who, at seven, are subintelligent or of average intelligence (cases of pronounced subnormality should be excluded from the general tables and entered in special tables, as such strong subnormality is obviously also connected with severe organic disturbance), then that could prove the importance of, if not heredity, at least the prenatal environment, and give an interesting sidelight on all the folklore that surrounds the behaviour of pregnant women.

Unfortunately, though, both my emotional as well as my economic circumstances prevent me from letting this experiment in the Hotel Orfila become the first in a series —long enough to be statistically valid—carried out by myself. And as Strindberg had to give up his dream of revolutionizing chemistry, I have to give up mine of revolutionizing psychology.

The rich man speaking about the joys of poverty was a figure that once used to appear in satire. As he was used he became a cliché. When he was recognized by the public as such he became ineffective as a figure. As he became ineffective he became unbelievable. The unbelievableness made him nonexistent.

Thus when K now speaks to me about the blessings of poverty I listen carefully. Contentment. Simple life. Food for the day. Unhappiness of wealth. I sit beside him while he drives his Cadillac through the slums of Delhi.

The impossibility of describing this situation: by being used in literature the reality has already been declared absurd, unrealistic and uninteresting.

How then describe K in a believable way? By lying. By the soft use of words. By understating him so that the reader almost, but not quite, gets the impression that K is a hypocrite. As you see, this is difficult. You don't believe what I said about K.

The autumn of 1959 and the spring of 1960 Gun and I lived in a house in Defence Colony on the outskirts of Delhi. First I was ill and in bed for some months, then Gun took care of me and the house and painted. Then I got better, then I wrote and Gun worked with the illustrations. During that time we also had a beautiful bitch. She had no degenerative race traits like the more purebred dogs we have had. She was a mongrel puppy we had picked up. We called her Wursti, semi-German for Little Sausage. I don't remember why.

Since I did not want her to beg for food at the table I had taught her that at the command "Good dog" she was not allowed to touch any food. I had to say "Now" in order to make her eat. Up to an hour might pass between the first and the second command. Meanwhile she guarded the food carefully against other dogs or strangers.

If she had found an old stinking bone I could also make her drop it by this command. She did not appreciate my taking it away from her. But she did not protest. "Good dog" thus became the signal for complete inhibition. Salivation ceased. She dropped whatever she had in her mouth—food, book, rug.

Later on she gave birth to three puppies. She was snappish and growling like all bitches immediately after delivery. When the last puppy was born and she was licking them clean I wanted to test the strength of the conditioned inhibition. I took away all three puppies and brought them out into the courtyard. Then I said:
—Good dog.

Wursti sat down at a safe distance from the three blind puppies who helplessly crawled over each other. Whimpering. Not until ten minutes later when I came back to the courtyard again did I say:
—Now.

Wursti went up to her puppies and carried them to the basket. Then she came up to me, licked my hand and wagged her tail. But she still snapped at everyone else who came near her.

This confirmed what I have always suspected. Maternal love, the strongest of instincts, is something very weak, easily blocked by any thoroughgoing conditioning. For a human being—who after all is a finely knit net of reflexes and inhibitions—it can, as instinct, be of hardly any importance whatsoever. That it seems to have become a conditioned reflex for most women in Western cultures to let parturition release a behaviour of semi-human type—give up active work, become something to be supported, sit in a "home" and read weeklies, have "female" interests—this is quite another thing. It must not be mistaken for maternal instinct. (As far as the maternal instinct is concerned the culture of the United States with its folkways of Caesarean operations, bottle feeding and mother stereotypes is of special interest.)

Now and then Gun and I used to visit the Westerners in their homes during their cocktail ceremonies. After listening to their conversation and observing the roles they were playing, we used to talk about the greater personal integrity of Wursti.

It should be added that we never did beat, maltreat or in other ways break the dog. Words, gestures, tone of voice were the signals we always used, both for impressing and releasing inhibitions and reflexes. Although the dog was gifted she could of course not speak or follow rationalized arguments, so we could not use the secondary signal system that is used for the conditioning of housewives and good citizens. This lack of ability to speak was thus the basis for the personal integrity of Wursti.

The monsoon is going to break any day now. I wake up in the morning. A big hunk of sweating meat. And I like it. And the air is like velvet in my lungs. From my bed I can see my typewriter standing on the white table. Gun is still asleep. I lie on my bed with all my meat sweating and suddenly I feel happy.

And the velvet is the stench from the open nullah and the taste of burning dung, and through the windows I can see the carrion-eating birds sitting on the rooftop looking towards me.

My friend N said:
—I married young. My wife wanted me to visit her family. I got dressed up and we took the train to the small provincial town where my father-in-law was the director of the insane asylum. When the train pulled in at the station my wife's sister was waiting on the platform. When we had left the train and stood on the platform she came running towards us. She may have been twenty-two at that time. She rushed up to my wife, then she looked at me, threw her hands to her face, covered her eyes and said, "No! No!" Thereupon she started to cry, embraced my wife and said, "You poor, poor thing." All the time I stood with our bag in my hand. I understood that it would not be easy to adjust to that family.

Oslo was at that time, the fall of 1945 and the spring of 1946, a strange town to starve in. (As had been Kristiania for Knut Hamsun.) My residence permit was cancelled. I was not able to prove that I had money enough to support me. I was suspected of working. My answer that nothing was more foreign to me—that I spent my days

in libraries and, sometimes, in cafés—gained no credence.
So I did not receive any further ration cards and I often
had to move because the authorities wanted to discuss
with me my residence permit, work, money and my being
in general.

In Oslo I became a human being. There I had intellectual intercourse with the left-wing socialists, myself
and world literature. (I also wrote poetry that nobody
wanted to publish and the poetry slowly filled up an old
shoebox.)

Rose-hip tea, ration-free ship biscuit, the smell of home-
grown tobacco, the books piled up, my typewriter
(Streamliner), a box full of poems, the wait for gift
parcels from Sweden and long dark streets, sleety, with
a sole streetlamp in the background.

Soon after I had visited Auschwitz, and while the
nausea still was strong, a nice and gentle Swedish engineer told me:

—There is so much propaganda. You never can trust
the Poles. And they are Communists. Remember that.
They have made it ghastly. And if the Jews were treated
that way they must have done something to the Germans.

I got upset. Because at that time I had illusions about
the nice and gentle people of our white Western culture.

But now I know that the nice people (the wellborn)
never find it very interesting to talk about (forgive and
forget, you know) the Jews, the Russians, the Poles
(there is so much propaganda) and all the others (and
by the way what could the Germans do with the Jews
and the Communists? They were at war. They had no
choice) who were gassed and got rid of with technical
efficiency. (And I spent my holidays in Germany last
summer and they said it had been a bad time but that
everything was quite exaggerated.)

Jews and Russians, Indians in Bengal, Chinese, Japanese and Negroes, ten million or more here or there, why should a decent Swede care? Of course it's too bad about the Asians but after all our ideals are the same. The world has to be made safe and we all, Americans, Swedes and Germans, are brothers. Aren't we?

As a child I read much. Also as an adolescent. But not until I became convinced that school was unnecessary did I get time to read seriously. Really systematic reading was possible only after I had been physically removed from (or left) school. In Stockholm, Karlstad, Oslo, Gothenburg and then again in Stockholm I bought books with every cent I could lay my hands on.

Then in the summer of 1946 I earned my living as a proofreader in Stockholm. I got credit in a secondhand bookshop, collected Strindberg and all the Swedish classics. I worked at night and lived in a room on Kungsholmen. Then I was thrown out by the landlady because girls visited me during the daytime.

—There must be order and decency.

Everywhere I lived I used to put up bookshelves and gather my books. But not until I moved to a cottage thirty-four miles west of Stockholm did my books become a library. At that time I had sixteen metres of books and when I had arranged them systematically I found that the systematization according to my own paths of association transformed the collection into a material memory.

Since then my library has grown at an average rate of seventy-five centimetres a month. Sometimes I suffered losses. I lost my whole Belgrade library, five metres, in the Hotel Majestic during my hurried departure from Yugoslavia in 1948. I had to sell eleven metres, most of it Swedish fiction, for bread and margarine in Gothenburg 1952 (when I was very hungry and very lean and the

Gothenburg poor-relief bureau refused to give me any help whatsoever:

—People like you, artists and suchlike, are the cancer of society, said the woman at the counter). I lost five metres of books stored in a Paris attic when the owner died. On the other hand Gun added some nineteen metres in October 1956. Thus gains and losses have cancelled each other out during the years.

I have not seen my library all in one place since Stockholm 1954. What has been added since then has been built up section by section in the towns where I have stayed. Then packed in boxes and sent somewhere. Mostly to Sweden. Now and then I hope to set up my library somewhere and work with it as a tool. I don't know when. I am not sure whether. It means a permanent residence. A library is like a child. A happy family. Which is rather fearsome.

It might thus seem as if there was something perverse behind this purchase of books. Paper in box after box stored in other people's attics in other towns. Anal fixation; the lust of ownership and gathering and holding back. After all, there are public libraries.

But it is not like that. My library is a memory. It works even when the books are in other places. I can close my eyes and see my library set up. See its different sections. That one in Stockholm, that one in Paris, that one in Berlin, that one in Delhi and so on. These different sections represent different fields of interest. They are marked by my particular consciousness at given times in given places. Thus my library for me still constitutes a whole. Put before a problem I only have to close my eyes, see the relevant section of the library, scan the shelves, see the titles and find the volumes that can give me a clue.

My visual memory is good. I never forget anything. (Except what I want to forget. Stupid people, uninteresting meetings.) Unfortunately it is not perfect. I cannot work like those who have a perfect photographic memory and can shut their eyes and read page after page. But I remember the typographical format of the text (the gestalt). I also remember the main lines of reasoning, see the notes and underlinings I have made myself, and thus I can work with a rather high degree of accuracy. Only the exact wording of the quotation and the spelling of names must always be checked. Spelling was never my strong point.

A public library cannot be used in the same way. It has been organized after other principles than mine. You seldom have the opportunity of getting to know the books in the library. You don't learn how they smell. (There is a fascinating difference between the smell of books from different countries and different printers. Blindfolded you can always smell if the book is English, Russian, American, Swedish and from what time it is. The glue, I suppose.) You can't hold them in your hands for a long time, feeling them. You can't underline and make notes in them. These three things are necessary if a library is to work as a memory. I must have arranged the books in such a way that the arguments (facts) fit in with my lines of reasoning. I must have had the physical, sensual experience of the book (the same difference as between getting to know a woman and just sleeping with her once or twice; the first woman you remember, for the second there is nothing to remember her by). And I must have worked with the book underlined, made marginal notes, cross references, written comments.

But if I have sold a book I find that it gets more and more difficult to make use of it. Usually I have had to remove as much as possible of the underlinings and comments in order to get a fair price for it. Also, in order to sell a book I must convince myself that the book is of no further use. After the sale I only get a hazy picture of it.

It has lost its natural place in my system, has entered new and strange connections. (That is what happened to the minor Swedish classics. I sold them and I lost them, slowly I am forgetting them. Thus I killed them.) Not the owning, but the system, the organized whole is important.

Of course I sometimes wonder whether this is just an expression of irrationality. A rationalization of the lust for ownership. Probably I could train myself to keep the book in my memory whatever happened to its physical presence. But that training would take effort. The choice then becomes a choice between that effort and the effort I have to make to balance the economic gain of selling books at secondhand bookstores. With the price they pay the choice is easy. The extra effort does not pay.

The fact that I am able to express (without finding it strange until it is long since written) even my memory in monetary terms shows how thoroughly debased I too have become in our consumer society. Nobody can transcend the social limits; ours is money.

—One day, says N, I wanted to put some order in my life. I started by organizing all my correspondence—including the love letters—in alphabetical and chronological order with proper index cards. It would make everything easier to survey, I thought. Since that time, though, love letters have ceased to arrive.

In February 1949 I had been standing outside of Vårgårda for six hours without getting a lift. I was going north and I was tired and hungry and the wind had been blowing over the frozen plains and I was cold. The snow whirled over the road in long coils and it was getting dark. My rucksack was icy, and all the time wind over the plains.

Finally I got a ride. But he was going to Herrljunga and I knew that Herrljunga was death. It was far to the side of the road. Only a railroad junction. I was very tired and the cabin of the truck was warm. I just couldn't get myself to give up the warmth. When the truck turned off from the main road I said nothing. Just sat. I came to Herrljunga at night. Snow whirling over the streets. I was tired and had two crowns and fifty öre. I went to a bar, bought a plain cup of coffee and two loose cigarettes. Warmed myself. Then I went out again. Looked for the police station. At that time I was often short of money and used to sleep in the police stations. They checked that you were not on the wanted list, checked your papers, took away your belt and locked you in a cell. Vagrancy (minor). It used to be warm. Though often full of lice. Sometimes they offered you coffee, sometimes they played cards with you.

The police station in Herrljunga was close to the tracks. It was a yellow wooden shack. (They probably were building a modern police palace, they were doing that all over Sweden then.) Three cells to the right, the office to the left.

—Sorry.

I was not allowed to stay there overnight. Nobody was on duty except when they had a prisoner. If I slept there the policeman had to stay up the whole night.

—Can't you find at least a drunk? I said.

—No, the policeman said. It's quiet tonight. I'm going home.

—Too bad, I said.

—Regulations, he said.

I went back to the railway station. Now it was really snowing. At the station a man wanted to buy my wedding ring for five crowns. He acted as if he thought I had stolen it. I didn't sell. I went back to the police station. It was empty. The door was open. The policeman had gone out to piss. I sneaked into the corridor, hurried to the cell farthest away and hid behind the open door. When I heard the policeman's steps I held my breath. He whistled, locked the door to his office, cleared his throat, locked the front door and was gone. I unrolled my sleeping bag on the bunk, unlaced my boots and put my trousers to press under the sleeping bag, then I snuggled down and fell asleep.

I woke up early, dressed, rolled up my sleeping bag and tied it under the rucksack, made myself ready to leave. Carefully I opened the cell door to the passage, but at the same moment the policeman opened the front door and saw me. He said:

—Hey you, what are you doing there?

Then he arrested me and I had to sit in the cell again. This time involuntarily. Finally I was allowed to call Stockholm. Gerard Bonnier of the Bonnier publishing house, who had no real reason to help me out (he had turned down my last poems), was kind enough to telegraph some money. He also spoke to the policeman.

When the money order arrived the policeman followed me until he saw that I got money. Then he took me home and his wife served meatballs and macaroni. They were decent to me. But he never let me out of sight for a minute. Finally he followed me to the train. There he advised me never to return to Herrljunga again. On the train the conductor entered my compartment every now and then. The policeman had spoken to him. I became worried about what was going to happen when we arrived in Stockholm. The authorities there were having one of their usual campaigns against vagrancy. So I jumped the train when it was slowing down to go through the freight yards on the South Side. It was snowing in Stockholm too. A couple of days later when I left Stockholm I got a ride just outside of Haga that took me all the way up to Sundsvall.

In the spring of 1960 we visited an American family. They are from Minnesota. They start to discuss religion.

I don't take part in the conversation. They intend neither to discuss the history of religion, the different religious beliefs nor the psychological and historical background of religious concepts. Finally they notice my silence and ask:

—What church do you belong to?

I answer truthfully that I don't belong to any. They seem surprised and ask if I am Jewish. I say that I don't belong to any religion. They ask what religion my parents belong to.

—As far as I know to none, I answer.

They all then start to ask questions about the religious life of my grandparents and great-grandparents and relatives. I do not like the discussion. They are friendly people and in their culture it is considered normal and laudable behaviour to ask personal questions. I also know that my growing irritation is only the result of my own upbringing in a culture where to ask such questions is considered a shameful insult. I keep my peace and try to get my eyes to look vacantly at them. I know that if I start a discussion about what interests me in religious beliefs and experiences this will cause unpleasantness, as they are culturally conditioned not to talk seriously about serious things and also culturally conditioned to regard their own mores as universally valid. But it is very unpleasant and I seek a way out.

—Don't you believe in anything? the woman asks.

—Not even that two and two make four? adds the man.

—Only under certain conditions is it true that two and two make four, I answer. (Because such is the truth.) But I also form my lips to a smile. Then they all smile back and we laugh pleasantly, with relief, and they are convinced that I am a joker.

In 1952 and 1953 I worked for long periods as an interpreter and translator. I also did some simultaneous interpreting. Sat with a headphone receiving one language while speaking another into a microphone. I sat in a glass cage. Felt like a converter. Have forgotten all the converted texts. The work was very trying. But it was probably a good mental discipline.

Tired and worn down after a period when I had had to work for twenty hours a day, I am now going north on a train. It is night and I am sitting in the upper berth in our sleeping compartment. The train is rocking. We are passing the mountains and I hear the steam engine, it sounds tired and old. There is soot everywhere. Under me F and C are sitting. We are all tired and have worked hard. They cannot talk directly to each other. They start telling folk tales. Automatically I interpret. After a while they begin to find the tales strange. They get queerer. F stands up and looks at me. I have fallen back on the pillow and am fast asleep. At the same time I mechanically continue saying some sentences in one language, make a pause, say some sentences in another language, make a pause, say some sentences in the first language. Then they give up telling folk tales.

In August 1956 I hitchhike up through France to visit my friends S and T. They live in the little town S. en Brie just outside Paris. The second day of my visit we go on a picnic. T packs a luncheon basket and S and I buy wine. Then we sit by the river eating, talking, drinking. We talk about other years and other friends. We come to speak about yoga. I take a lotus position. Thereafter I coil myself into a ball, lock my head between my interlocked legs and start to turn somersaults. It looks very peculiar and never fails to produce a certain effect. I walk around on my kneecaps and elbows. I feel gay. I turn somersault upon somersault, bouncing like a rubber ball. T laughs. Then I turn four quick somersaults backwards. But I have misjudged the distance to the river bank and while my brain is still spinning in the somersaults I notice that my elbows do not make any contact with the ground after the fourth. I understand something has gone wrong.

Like a ball I roll down the steep slope. I am unable to get out of the knot into which I have twisted myself. I roll faster and faster and suddenly I disappear under water. I hold my breath and struggle to get free. Just as I have been able to untie myself and get my head above water and draw breath S comes sliding down the slope. He helps me up. A train passes on the railway bridge. Slowly I work my way up the slippery and high river bank. I shake myself to get rid of the water and T pours wine in my glass. Just where I struck the water a stone juts out. I see that my head missed it by less than two centimetres. We all laugh and drink.

In 1959, in Kabul, I met quite a number of Westerners. Many of them irritated me. They were so contemptuous of the Afghans for religious reasons. They could talk for hours about the barbarity of Islam. In order to give them a perspective on their own religion I tried to ask:

—What do you think the normal Afghan thinks of a religion whose adherents ritually eat up their god at regular intervals?

But this question failed to produce an effect. They never even reacted. At first I thought it was because they failed to see their own behaviour from without. Later on, however, I understood that they simply knew nothing about the discussions of transubstantiation and consubstantiation in Christianity. They had no understanding of the holiness of their rites. This confirmed what I had observed as a child during the divinity lessons of my school days.

.   .   .

I worked at a Chinese circus. On stage I wore a tuxedo and introduced the acts:

—Ladies and gentlemen, it is indeed an honour . . .

For the rest I was a combined stagehand and sub-impresario. We gave two performances every night, the house was usually quite full, in many places we were the only entertainment that winter.

One of the acts was jug-dancing. You know, two elderly men and beautiful chinaware jugs. They handled them as if they were made of balsa wood. Without apparent effort they threw the jugs in the air, caught them on their heads and danced. Only if you stood close could you see the strain of the art in their eyes and see them sweating. To the public it was just a beautiful circus act.

In the interval, as well as in the pause between the performances, they used to have one of the young boys from the acrobat family along. They were training him. They were friendly and the boy worked hard.

Two minutes before the show was to open—the orchestra had already started playing—for the first of our performances in Skara the boy dropped one of the jugs. A harsh, jingling sound. Everybody was quiet. The boy fetched a broom and a dustpan and began sweeping.

—Bad luck! said the oldest jug-dancer.

In the interval I observed that the jug-dancers gave the boy a jug. The boy swept it off ground with his right arm and started dancing.

—How dare they? I asked the bicycle equilibrist who was standing beside me and drinking beer. They have only got three jugs left.

—The boy must learn, he said. You see, if he doesn't continue his training today he will never make it. He will be a failure. If he drops that jug too they will have to change their act, I suppose.

The boy never dropped the jug again. After three months he sometimes was allowed to appear on stage as their assistant.

One day in September 1945 Reidar asks me if I want to go along on a trip. They are going to search the house of a man who had collaborated with the Germans, a member of Quisling's party. We drive there in a truck. Two soldiers (or at least men in uniform) ride along with us. We drive through the suburbs of Oslo. When we stop and get off we have to go up a well-kept gravel path up to the house. On the lawn white stones are placed in nice patterns and a stable lantern is mounted on the gatepost. We knock and a balding man opens the door. He bows deeply to us. Bows several times. He bows like a waiter in a bad comedy. His skin is yellow and he sweats. He thinks we are going to shoot him. I poke a finger in his chest and say:
—Boof!
We all laugh. He laughs loudest. We enter the garage. All the time he shows us the way. He utters clicking sounds in his throat. Bows and smiles. We load the truck full with banners and papers. The man hears that I am Swedish. He gives me a party rubber stamp and an Iron Cross. When we leave he stands in the doorway. I notice that he has a small paunch and green braces. His house is newly painted.
—I wonder where he stole that, says Reidar about the Iron Cross.

In 1941 our divinity teacher, a young man fresh from the theological faculty of Uppsala University, warned us against secret vices. This irritated me. I considered him unsound and unscientific. Therefore I made a statistical research on the sexual habits of the students of our class, the I⁴B coeducational class of Bromma Secondary School. He blushed crimson when I delivered the results to him.

All of us masturbated. All the boys had been masturbating since they were eight or nine. The same with the girls. All of them masturbated, they said, except two who said "No" and then giggled and one who gave me a box on the ear and started to cry when I asked her. We were fourteen and masturbated like monkeys in a zoo.

In the fall of 1935 I was transferred to Ålsten Primary School. I was in the second grade at the time. At the beginning of October—I still remember that it was sunshine and summer in the air that day—the teacher lectured us on Christianity. Next hour—I don't remember in what connection—the words "celestial bodies" cropped up in the text we were reading. She asked us children if we could say what the celestial bodies were. A girl from a religious home immediately answered, "Angels." The teacher got very upset. The girl was expelled from the classroom and we children all laughed.

I spent the summers immediately before the Second World War with my maternal uncles. They then leased a farm in Kvicksta from my maternal grandfather. They were young, younger than I am now. They had old cars which they repaired. They had lots of dogs. There is a feeling of sunlight and a scent of hay around these summers. The humming of flies and the feeling of wet moss between my toes deep in the forest, the shower of sparks from the wire sockets when there was a thunderstorm and lightning struck the transformer.

When they worked in the forest I could follow them. Nobody ever asked me about anything, but nobody was irritated if I asked. It is true that I was not allowed to piss on the floor or chew rugs, but then neither were the dogs. I slept when I wanted, got up when it pleased me and went to bed when I got tired. Nobody cared when I had smashed my knee and nobody asked any questions when I crawled around in the attic looking for old inner tubes to repair and float on in the lake.

Those are the only childhood days that I look back to with any feeling of pleasure. The peace and quiet of them is best described by quoting my paternal aunt who, when I came back from Kvicksta in the autumn, screamed:

—Have you gone barefoot without washing your feet for two months!

And then put me in a bathtub, scrubbed hard and talked of the social need for cleanliness and discipline.

I am not exactly a kin-loving man. When I think about kinship systems and my kindred my skin begins to prickle and I can feel my neck-hair rising. A physical discomfort before a latent threat to my individuality. You get born into a kinship net, a collective not chosen by yourself, a collective where you are the youngest, the one everybody has the right (duty) to educate, reprove, urge on. The dream of the well-adjusted family member: to become so adult and get a mother so ancient and weak that he can say:

—Oh no, mother dear, vermouth is bad for you, and take the glass out of her hand while all the kindred look on and smile pleasantly.

Not until very late did I understand in what social and historical situation this attitude of mine had been moulded. For a long time I regarded my own feelings as a general truth. Now I know that they are but subjective reactions to a certain situation.

On my mother's side the family comes from the Mälar region. It is no clan. They may not meet for ten years at a time, maybe not more than once or twice in a lifetime. When they meet they are in general friendly. A couple of years ago I discovered that I did not regard them as

kin, just as nice and kind people I knew (and to whom
I had certain special relationships). They are scattered
around Lake Mälar and I might visit them someday.

But on my father's side the family comes from Dalecarlia. Petty peasants, millers, Finnish sharecroppers, even
tinkers. But all of them—as far back as I know—from the
same village. If inbreeding was genetically bad we would
all be morons. Looking back behind me they line up in row
upon row back to medieval times, all of them poor, most
of them sullen and sour, born, breaking land, working it,
dying, none of them ever well known. None of them ever
a hero. And until the last generation none of them ever
breaking the bonds of the village. There is kin and kin
and even if the rest of Sweden redistributed the village
lands nearly two centuries ago we have not done it yet.

The living members of that family still constitute a
living organism. They are like most Swedes. City dwellers,
some are intelligent and some stupid, some are alcoholics
and some are religious, some have had success and some
have failed and are dissatisfied with their lives. But they
all live within the kinship system. In my father's generation they are one—or rather a half—generation away
from the soil of the Myres, the Knuts, the Perers, the Bus,
the Mickels, the village.

It was my paternal grandfather and his brothers who
broke away from the village and went into town. But his
life was one of land hunger and he died (broke) as a
farmer in Södermanland. But the family that has become
urbanized and occupies a place in the middle of the social
pyramid still lives inside the constricted soil-bound kinship
that was natural in the village where the land was never
redistributed. From a Continental, or British, viewpoint
one might say that we still have not really climbed out
of the early middle ages.

It was in the conflict between these two completely

different family structures that I—in my own position as someone born in the city—could come to see this tight kinship net as something negative. It no longer has any social function. It is just the heavy corpse of a dead peasant society. But the experience of this type of family has made it possible for me to read Russian classics and Balzac.

I am seven and I am spreading butter on a piece of rye crisp. Someone says:

—It is not difficult to tell who your mother is. She and her family have never learnt how to distinguish the right side of the bread from the wrong side.

I am fourteen. My parents are abroad. My sisters, seven and five, are not baptized. The intention was that they should decide for themselves when they got older whether they wanted to belong to any church. Now the family descends on us, the aunts, the uncles, the second cousins, and they fetch my sisters despite my violent protests. They take my sisters down to Norrköping where one of my paternal uncles is headmaster of a school. There they call in the parson and my sisters are forcibly baptized. Afterwards Sissela told me she had refused to wash before the ceremony. They had had to hold her. It was no public scandal, it was all kept in the family.

In November 1960 I publish a book on Afghanistan in Swedish. A relative who is a librarian and responsible for the purchase of books sends me word:

—There are things written in that book that are not fit for the family.

I rack my brains over what I can have written about Afghanistan that is unfit for the family.

February 1948. I am going by train from Sarajevo to Belgrade. The journey takes thirty-six hours and the cars are crowded. People hang like grape clusters at the doors.

They make room for me. I am a foreigner. They push me
and press me into a compartment. They pull in their legs so
I can sit on my typewriter case. It is snowing and the
sky is grey. There is a cold draught because the car has no
windowpanes. Although we are jammed tight the breath
curls like smoke from our mouths. There are many tunnels
and the man who speaks German tells about the art of
blowing up bridges.

Three peasants on their way to a conference in Belgrade
bring out their provisions. They offer us food. Thick black
bread and cubes of hard smoked fat pork. Later on the
train is less crowded. I stand in the corridor looking out.
The hills are nude under the snow. In the night I can sleep
in the corridor. I have wrapped my raincoat around my
body and sleep deeply. Wake up, numb, shivering. It is
dark, a girl is singing. I can see her in silhouette against the
window. A man leans down to me and offers me a cigarette.
When he lights the match I see that he has a scar on his
left cheek.

My son is eleven. I have just come to Sweden from
three years in Asia. It is December 1960 and I am planning
to go away again and stay away for several years more.
He will be fourteen or fifteen the next time I see him. I
remember him as a baby; changing diapers. I get no contact. Very little of what is mine am I able to convey to
him. I try to talk to him about the world and the wars,
about the high mountains, the deserts, the Turkomans on
their horses; try to fit into a children's book world. I fail.

For a moment I feel misunderstood by my son and would
like to do something about it. Then I laugh. It strikes me
that he is a being of his own. I can no more speak to him
and expect to be understood than my father could speak
to me or his father to him.

I remember myself at eleven, remember the unbridgeable gap to the elders, look at my son who is stubbornly busying himself with his stamps, and forever give up trying to say to him something in particular. Then I say goodbye and go down to my ship.

In August 1955 I have followed M to the Gare du Nord. It is a hot day and she is leaving now.

—Take care of yourself, I say.

She tries to lean out of the window and say something but the train is already leaving and I don't hear her, I wave my hand. I am all alone and there is a summery peace around me. I go to a bar. I take a calvados. Then I take one more and move on homewards.

I am alone. Sitting at my window, reading. I drink my coffee in the morning. Go down to the next street and buy bread and cheese. Comfortable, solitude all around. My friends have left town. In August Paris is a deep pleasant loneliness around me. Suddenly I have plenty of time, I read, I work. The days are all mine and I am happy.

To the very last moment: emotions, scenes, words. But when I see M in the train window and am happily unable to hear what she is saying and the train pulls out, I know that these four years are over now. All at once the back-drop has changed, the scene is different and a train is leaving Paris and people are shouting and waving their hands and my hand too is waving and a beautiful girl leans out of a window and shouts something I don't have to hear and she cries, I see, and everything I said just two minutes ago is now irrelevant. On drinking my calvados I suddenly notice that M is gone and that I don't even miss her any more and I wonder a little bit about how fast one can switch on and off.

When M comes back to Paris six weeks later I don't know how to explain it to her. I can't just say that suddenly the stage was reset the moment the train pulled out and she travelled right out of my life. There is no other woman. There is no other reason than that all my emotions had become worn down and suddenly snapped. I am sitting in my room writing. Then I walk to the kitchen and smile kindly at M over my coffee. All the time the lust for work and solitude and the lonely stillness itching through my body. But I smile kindly at her and I see that her beautiful lips are moving and she is saying something, but I don't hear her any more and just smile.

In the autumn of 1946 a series of explosions occurred in Stockholm. The first ones hardly attracted any attention. Were treated in one column, inside page. But when the bombs continued to explode in different parts of the city, preferably on Saturdays, the unknown perpetrator attained front-page headlines and was called the "Sabbath saboteur." The public was warned to be on guard against suspicious characters.

I myself was at that time rather uninterested in the Sabbath saboteur. I lived in a cottage (owned by the Church of Sweden, by the way) at Tingsviken at Lejondal near Bro just northwest of Stockholm. I wrote poems and gathered mushrooms. My poems were to change the world; they were never published though. But the mushrooms were eatable. Furthermore I was in love.

The girl I lived with and was in love with one day told me that she had to go to Stockholm. She worked (had worked rather) in an office, but was going to become an actress, had had bit parts and was to go to a theatre school. She was nineteen. Two days after she had left I got a letter from her. She had left me. "As you must have understood." I had understood nothing of the kind. I became unhappy and agitated. Wrote a long letter to her, explaining why she in reality did not want to leave me "after all." This letter of mine was just as bombastically false as letters from disappointed lovers suffering from deep emotion usually are. I know—at that time I made carbon copies of all my letters and half a year ago I happened to find it when I was burning bad manuscripts and unnecessary papers.

Since I got no answer to my letter I cycled down to Bro, returned empty beer bottles to the grocery store and took the train to Stockholm. There I went to see the girl. I found her at the theatre school. First she laughed at me, then she was full of sympathy. She cried with sympathy for me. One is always sympathetic at that age and in that situation. But such was her life and such was my life and even if I felt hurt I must understand that she was in love with another man and gloriously happy as never before in her whole life.

When I got out on the street again I started to weep. Later on I found myself not far from the old observatory. People were looking at me and as I was afraid that someone would start talking to me and try to help me, I wanted to hide. I had come directly from the cottage and was dressed as I was accustomed to. Green surplus trousers tucked down in high (muddy and black) rubber boots, a chequered lumber jacket, and a red bandanna around my neck. My face was swollen and red from crying. I found a telephone booth and took refuge in it. I called my friend D and talked about how life and love were hell. He was understanding. Suddenly the door was thrown open. A middle-aged couple pointed their right-hand forefingers at me and shouted in unison:

—There he is!

Two policemen seized hold of me and pulled me from the telephone and out of the booth.

—Now we have you, one of them said.

Lots of people crowded around us and I understood nothing. They were all shouting. I was taken to the police station. I don't even remember if the sirens were on. I only remember that I was held in a tight grip. I was searched from head to foot and locked up in a cell.

After a while I was taken to the police sergeant. He sat reading the carbon copy of my letter to the girl. I had kept it in the pocket of my lumber jacket.

—You like Strindberg? he suddenly asked.

—Yes, I said.

—Have you read *Married*?

—Yes.

—Do you like it?

—Yes.

—Why?

I tried to explain why I considered *Married* a great book. I also regarded *Black Banners* as a great book, explained why.

The police sergeant grew dark.

—Do you share the Strindberg philosophy?

—That depends, I said. I don't know if you could say he had any coherent ideology. But in the main I suppose I share his feelings. I don't think I will end up, become religious, though, like he did.

—So you are against religion? Are you against marriage too? What is your attitude towards the Royal Family?

By now I was all confused. The police sergeant watched me in silence for a long time, then he ordered me taken back to the cell. Up to that moment I had been paralyzed by unhappy love and wounded self-esteem, had regarded the police hearing as a "written" ending to my love. But now that I sat on the bunk and suddenly realized that I indeed was sitting locked up in a cell being accused of something—I never knew what—that had to do with Strindberg and *Married*, I felt panicky.

I was taken to a new hearing. This time the interrogation concerned Almquist. The police sergeant was an educated man. Sometimes I tried to give intelligent answers to his questions. No, I did not believe that Almquist really had tried to poison the moneylender even if it was difficult to prove his innocence.

—He ran away, said the police sergeant.

—But that was in 1851, I said. You know how our courts were working at that time. Almquist was a very hated man, he was a good writer and he was afraid of being framed so he fled the country.

—So, said the police sergeant. You defend crime.

When I tried to ask him what it was all about he just answered:

—You will hear in due time.

He started on Villon, he continued with Tolstoy. I felt the panic increase. Whatever I said was turned against me. I wondered whether I was experiencing a hallucination. (Maybe I am getting schizophrenic, I thought.) I leaned forward and touched the arm of the police sergeant. He was real, though, and snapped at me:

—Don't you try any tricks here.

The net was tightening around me. He interrogated me about Marx and Bakunin, Stirner and Kropotkin. He wondered about my attitude towards mankind and society.

Suddenly the interrogation was broken off. He was called to the telephone. He came back. Told me that I could leave. Shook hands. When I left the station I heard that the Sabbath saboteur had been caught. He had confessed. I am still deeply convinced that if he had not been caught I would have had to spend the next few years locked up in a cell. My absolute innocence and the confusion with which that innocence stamped me only tended to make me more guilty. The interrogation had brought forth answers that only strengthened the police sergeant's conviction of the harmfulness of literature. Who knows, by the way, if I wouldn't have confessed to anything just to get away from this nightmare life of sitting in a cell wondering why I was there only to be taken out and interrogated about Strindberg, Almquist and Villon.

After this I often wonder how many actually are guilty. And if they are guilty, what they are guilty of. Maybe some poor devil is now sitting in Härnösand because he stumbled over Leo or tripped up over Feodor and now—the murdered murdered and the murderer missing—is locked up for his literary blunders.

There is a cold wind blowing this morning. The summer is coming; the ice on the lake has broken and the forest on the far side is a violet haze of young birches. From where I sit I follow a sea gull with my eyes. There is glass between us. I hear the wind. My house has been built between the forest and the lake in a nice and peaceful country.

I live in the best of worlds. If I had the guts I would walk down the corridor on the right-hand side, open the door to the guest room, take down the (conversation piece for visitors) kukri from the wall and slit my throat. But I don't have the guts. And just by writing this I turn the thought into (bad) literature.

I don't see much reason to exist. My words turn to lies the moment they are uttered. They crawl over the pages of books and newspapers. I get letters from bankers and politicians saying how much they like me. Everything I write, everything I do seems to serve the niceness and order of this peaceful country in this the best of worlds.

Eating my breakfast, coffee, toast and cheese, reading my morning paper I suddenly look up and see my reflection in the windowpane and I remember how the SS officers, the cultured ones, sat in small villages in Poland at night filling their diaries with thoughts about Goethe and Hegel, *Weltgeist* and life, substance and soul and Beethoven after their day's work had been done.

Like them I am an ordinary European caught in a web of lies and traditions and realities. But unlike them I held —and hold—that they should die for their crimes. Whatever their motives. Thinking this I eat my toast and the cheese is strong and well aged.

It was in 1957. I was in my thirtieth year. A European and a writer, citizen of a small country on the northwestern fringe of the Eurasian continent. I had been drifting about all over Europe—east and west—since the war ended twelve years before. Worked at this and that: on newspapers, in offices, at a circus, handling freight on the railroad, testing loudspeakers in a radio factory; but most of the time just writing. Now I had published my fifth book, a novel, my fourth novel, and the winter was turning cold along the streets of Stockholm.

We had just returned to Sweden, Gun and I. We had been in Spain. Together with a painter and a sculptress from Stockholm we had there rented a small house outside of a town called Nerja on the Andalusian coast between Málaga and Almuñecar. Spain was poor. The tourists at that time had not advanced north of Málaga. So we lived and worked in Spain since we could not afford to live in Sweden. From Nerja we had gone to Paris. They no longer had a special glass reserved for me at the tabac. But I took a calvados and the people crowding the bar were the same as in former years. When I left the tabac I met Roger at Place Saint-Michel. We talked about Hungary and the role of the Left in Europe. He had moved to Villejuif, he said. From Paris we had gone to Moscow. Pavel told me they were considering translating one of my novels into Russian. (They did, too, in 1960.) At the House of Writers I met a poet who was said to be a very promising writer about the revolution that occurred in Russia fifteen years before he was born. But I never saw his face. It was in the basement lavatory; he was kneeling, hugging the toilet and spewing with his head in the hole. But the hope of revolutionary literature had grey pants.

The novel I had written in Spain was the one just published. It was a funny novel. (I still like it.) At least it was said to be comical. A burlesque about love in the suburbs. The main character committed suicide in the last chapter and I got a prize. The moment I had cashed my check from the State Literary Fund that afternoon I went to the Golden Peace restaurant in the Old Town. It is not a bad place to go to. It's owned by the Swedish Academy. You know, the institution that gives Churchill and Sully-Prudhomme, Sholokov and Kipling and other world champions of writing "in an idealistic vein" literary Nobel prizes. I have sometimes in foreign countries heard the "o" stressed. That is wrong, the "e" should be stressed.

People used to meet at this restaurant. Many still do. The people in this case are the writers, the editors, the critics, the painters and the actors. It was like a club. You felt good and "in" going there. The tourists sat in the cellar downstairs (medieval atmosphere), we sat upstairs. If the tourists wanted to sit upstairs, then they were told that all tables had been reserved. I remember that I had been allowed to sit upstairs in 1953. Now we were all sitting here. It was good knowing each other.

I was drinking heavily and there were a lot of people coming and going. We all talked. Girls, sputniks, socialism, Hungary, art, editors, how to organize criticism and who knows what about whom. Later on that evening Gun came. She had been putting up an exhibition. I continued drinking and in some way I tried to tell myself that everything was shaping up. Money and good criticism and all that. Five years earlier I had had to go to the pawnbroker with my typewriter just to get money to stay alive. Even two years ago I had been so damned hungry when I wrote that novel that it had five chapters just describing food. A sort of gastric pornography. One of the chapters was devoted to the sight of fresh young spring potatoes boiled in salt water.

At the table next to mine one of the poets of the elder generation, a man soon to die—but that neither he nor I knew—leaned over to me, nearly spilling his glass of whisky, grabbed my arm and said:

—Why are you such a damnably bad writer? You and all of your generation. You have to write with your heart's blood. Our generation struggled.

He got agitated. Talked about Spain. He had once had plans to go as a volunteer, he said. But he never made it. He just wrote about the Republic instead. He shook me hard and said:

—What are we? What are you, what am I? The arse-lickers of the powerful, the mighty, the cultured. Betrayed betrayers of the ever betrayed.

Then he really spilled his glass. When he got a new one he started singing:

> *Marcháos, legionarios*
> *marcháos, hitlerianos*
> *¡ay mamita mía!*
> *a vuestra tierra*
> *porque el proletariado*
> *¡ay mamita mía!*
> *ganó la guerra . . .*

I tried to tell him that they did not win the war and that the hitlerianos of Spain were making the country into the playground of the Swedish proletariat. One could not very well sing of the victory of the Swedish workers winning summer resorts in Spain. But he did not listen any more. He had a rather beautiful blonde at his table.

I knew her. She was talking softly to him, calming him. She stroked his arm and talked about poetry.

—You are so beautiful, I heard him say.

He later wrote a good review of her poems. She was a good writer.

To me 1957 was a good year. Five more years and I would be in all the encyclopedias (Swedish), fifteen more years and I would have secured my niche in the history of Swedish literature. This was the future that glistened and tinkled the ice in my Scotch and soda.

The more I drank, the more attractive the girls became. They were always the same, sitting at different tables different nights. And we were the same. They never got beautiful until we got drunk. And we didn't get attractive until they got drunk. Out of this we got raw material for incisive books about love. Gun said:

—If I throw a hand grenade here Sweden will have lost her culture.

I remember her saying this because there was a lull in the conversation and her remark floated out over the restaurant and there was a moment of quietness before the voices once more rose protectively around all of us.

There was a long discussion about alienation and literature. At 2 A.M. we were thrown out. They turned off the lights. Then they started taking away the chairs. At the end they led us to the door. They were nice about it. They always were. I was drunk. The streets were narrow, winding, there were walls everywhere. The cold stone wall grew up against my hands, as my head jerked back I found my eyes looking upwards, the strip of sky was very clear around the chimneys and in the cold winter night, the stars were coming close and I fell. Gun managed to get me home that night. I crawled up the stairs on all four legs. Like a dog, panting. She dragged me up on the bed and undressed me. I heard my shoes falling to the floor and she wrapped a woollen blanket around me. Next day I had a hangover, but drank two bottles of beer and wrote an essay about the role of the Eulenspiegel figure in the German peasant war. Not the De Coster Eulenspiegel, but the folk hero. The idea being of course that the crudity of Eulenspiegel and Simplex was the only reasonable way of describing the reality today.

Yes, in my thirtieth year I was—doubtingly—planning to continue telling stories for Swedes; knowing that the book-buying and book-reading public of Sweden were just those honourable people that Eulenspiegel farted on. But as a European of my generation I had drunk my fill of shame. I had got a gold filling in a lower left molar in 1944. Germany had paid for Swedish exports with gold at that time. I often wonder whose tooth that is chewing in my mouth. A Jew from Lodz, or one from Amsterdam?

At the time when I had finished my crudity about love in the suburbs and we were to leave Spain, we had a big party. One of our friends, a Swedish painter, then managed to sneak into the Guardia Civil headquarters. He reached the communications centre and as he had been a tele-graphist in the Swedish army he sent an emergency message along the open line. It was relayed all along the east coast of Spain:

```
·—·—·—·—·—  ·—·—·—·—·—  ·—·—·—·—  · ·—·—
·—· ·——·——·—·——· ·—· —·—·· ·—·· ·——·——· ·——· ·
·—· ·——· ·—··—·——· ·—·——·——· ·—··—··—·——· ·
```

Thus the tickers in the security headquarters that night were punching out his warning to the guardians of Franco. A message in the unreadable language of Swedish:

ATTENTION ATTENTION ATTENTION EUROPE
NEEDS MORE SAUSAGE END OF MESSAGE

Like him and like all of us I was neither wholly foolish nor wholly wise. But I knew that something was deeply wrong. And a month after the day when I had written about the Eulenspiegel figure and Gun had opened her exhibition we drove southwards, out of Europe, in a 2CV Citroën. It would be several years before we returned. Though we didn't know that. When we returned we would be quite different.

So it was in my thirtieth year, when I had drunk out of my shame as a European but was neither wholly foolish nor wholly wise. Now the snows of that winter of 1957 are long since gone.

HANUMANGARH, October 12—A group of labourers employed on the Rajasthan Canal employed a novel method of placing their grievances before Vice-President Radhakrishnan when he came to the site to release the water from the canal yesterday.

About fifty labourers marched in procession carrying colourful bunting fixed on bamboo sticks and occupied the front row among the audience.

Just after the Vice-President's speech the labourers quietly replaced the bunting by petitions which they had in their pockets and started waving to draw Dr. Radhakrishnan's attention. Policemen in white clothes immediately snatched their petitions.

Each petition bore the thumb impressions of about fifty labourers narrating their tales of woe and demanding their wages which, they alleged, had not been paid for several months.

Before leaving for Jaipur, Mr. Ram Chander, Minister for the Rajasthan Canal, told this correspondent that he had asked the labourers to hand over the petitions to him so that he could inquire into the matter.

The Hindustan Times, October 13, 1961

If this is reality, which description will not be betrayal? A sociological study will tell how the workers were recruited. How their families live. The scene in Hanumangarh on October 11, 1961, will be dissolved into chapters and statistical tables and . . . objectively speaking, the circumstances . . . The scientist will have inquired into the matter. Our libraries are filled with the results of these inquiries. It is a nice and scientific way of putting the bunting back.

Of course one can transform the plight of the canal workers into art. Sentimental descriptions of Asian poverty always appeal to the middle classes of both Western and Eastern countries. And after all they are the ones who buy the books. Or one can make social and agitational drama out of it. A stagehand holds up a sign: THE WATER IS RELEASED. EVERYBODY IS HAPPY. Vice-President (white turban, saintly smile) sitting on high-backed chair on dais to the left of stage. Workers in dhotis and red turbans (Rajasthanis have red turbans) squatting in front of dais. Each worker carrying bamboo stick with colourful bunting. All smiling trustfully (it seems) at Vice-President high on dais. From right advance policemen in white uniforms in British slow march led by Punjabi piper in kilt and turban. Foresinger addressing the audience:

High are the mighty
far away
When close to you
difficult to reach
When talking to you
hard of hearing
Graceful are the mighty
leaning towards you
When you lean back
seeking support

you fall
See now how the workers of Hanumangarh . . .

The aesthetic effect can be discussed. But in any case
the audience will be pleasantly reassured of its intellectual
superiority. Poor damn devils of Hanumangarh, trusting,
not knowing better.

The correspondent expressed it clearer. But to whom?
How many readers reacted? And how did they show their
reaction?

I believe it was Louis Jouvet—the great actor—to
whom a girl wanting to become an actress said:

—You see, I feel so much.

And he replied:

—But my dear lady, it is not you but the audience that
should feel.

I am a writer, a mixer of words, a user of phrases, but
I distrust my tools.

Stapled to the clipping from *The Hindustan Times* is a
yellow foolscap with a few lines of writing:

"Describe destruction of human solidarity through the
spreading of (true) information. Saturation, satiation,
negation.

"Saw a corpse in the gutter outside the house on Hard-
ing Avenue one spring morning in 1959. Saw it the whole
day. Found myself irritated by the thought that it was
beginning to smell."

It ought to be noted that there was a rational reason
too: I was afraid that I was going to be charged with the
funeral expenses. And I was short of money. The next
evening the corpse was gone. I don't know what happened
to it.

Herat is a beautiful town. I have seen the Timurid
monuments of Samarkand. But nowhere a cupola such as

that of the mausoleum of Gohar Shad, wife of Shah Rukh. Herat would have been a still more beautiful town if the British had not blown up the great Musallah. It had been built on the orders of Gohar Shad by the great architect Quavam ad-Din. The construction was begun in 1417. It was the grandest monument of the Timurid era. It was blown up in 1885. The British needed a clear field for their cannon in the war with Russia that never came.

Walking over the field, trampling on the debris, crushing decayed tilework with my heels seventy-three years after the dynamiting, I feel a hatred sour as green gall filling my mouth. The queen and the tsar are both dead and gone. So are all their generals and merchants, poets,

> (Kabul town was ours to take—
> Blow the bugle, draw the sword
> Kabul town'll go to hell—
> Blow the bugle, draw the sword)

journalists and diplomats. But their work remains. The ugliest, dirtiest, most boastful and unglorious culture the world has ever had to bear. Their bodies might be dead, the queens and tsars, but their spirits still march beside us through the most murderous century in history. But we should not say this. We should be nice and well behaved. Talk about understanding, the modern world, man, or rather Man.

I wrote about the Musallah. Not quite as sharp as this. More descriptive. More pacific. And then I found out that I seemed to be the only one who had reacted in this way. The only European, I mean. The Afghans have felt this way the whole time. And coming back to Kabul in 1961 I met a Norwegian expert who said to me:

—It might be true. But you should not write it. You are disloyal to Europe.

And I understood why the others did not react. Europeans never react. Except when natives go European and repay some minor atrocities. (By Europeans I mean Europeans all the way from the Urals to California.)

Yes, it was in Herat that I became conscious of being disloyal to Europe. That my values had shifted and that I felt loyalty to Europe to be a crime. It was the German who helped me. The German more than the debris of the Musallah.

We had been in Herat two days when I met him one afternoon in July 1958. I had been cleaning the carburetor of our car. Thinking about the cold war of 1885. "The big game" as it was called. That war never became a hot war. But waging it cold they managed to dynamite Herat. It seemed like I had heard similar things in my own time.

Afterwards I sat in the shade of the pines beside the pool in front of the old Herat Hotel drinking green tea. I was hot and sweating. We were going to drive northwards the next morning. I saw him coming. A lean man around forty. Maybe older. First I thought he was an Afghan. He was so dressed. Then he sat down beside me and said in English:

—You are a European.

He spoke English with a slight accent; but spoke a good public school English.

—Good to see a European again. I have been up north these last months. I am a German.

I told him I was a Swede. He asked me if I spoke German. I did, so we continued in German. He was an officer, he said. Or rather a former officer. He had been a staff officer.

—My uncle was on the general staff.

Later on that evening he began speaking about the north. He had been up to the border, he said.

—I have many friends.

I could not quite decide whether he was real or not. A phony spy or a real one. He had notebooks filled with facts. They seemed to contain a full military topography of northern Afghanistan.

—I also have got all the Soviet airstrips just across the border, he said.

He talked about his friends in Kabul. He was worried. He did not dare to write to them.

—Not even to the embassy, you know. The Afghans check everything. You can't trust them. You can't even trust the people. You should never send a letter in this country.

He wanted me to carry some letters for him to Kabul. I refused. That surprised him.

—But I never do, I said.

He was quiet a moment. Then he talked of girls in Berlin. He was a nice chap. An hour later he once more asked me to carry the letters. It was very important to him. I still refused.

—Then I will try to reach the border, he said. But the Afghans check everything.

Then he left. It was now quite dark and the kerosene lamp I had borrowed made a small yellow globe of circling insects in the night. I went to bed and early next morning we started north for the Sabzak Pass.

When we arrived in Kabul I thought about the German. He seemed to have been a nice, middle-aged man. A fool maybe. But I disliked the idea of German (if it was German) espionage (if it was espionage) in the Afghan north. I thus decided to take the matter up with the Afghan authorities. I told the story of the German at a party, I gave all the details but I put the story in the form of an anecdote.

Abdul smiled and said:

—Oh yes, we know all about him. We did all along. We usually do. That has already been taken care of.

Then we both laughed. The American I had been drinking beer with at the International Club stared at me. Then he edged away. He looked as if he had seen a snake.

I know why. The German had trusted me because I was a European. The American felt that I was a traitor to Europe. As for myself, I understood that I had passed one of the gates to Asia. My loyalty was no longer an unquestioned loyalty to Europe. And I was quite prepared to let the Afghans take care of (whatever that meant) the German who had been collecting military information in their country.

In January 1959 we had been driving from Bombay. We were on our way to Delhi. But we were not driving the grand trunk road; we were crisscrossing from monument to monument. This night we had come from Ajanta and the next morning we were to go to Mandu. We slept in the dak bungalow at Dhulia and the khansamah prepared food for us. Or rather, the khansamah gave us a British meal. Like a crime committed this meal would immediately be forgotten—driving towards Mandu I didn't give it a thought—but would then reappear and haunt me for several years. The eating of this meal in Dhulia was one of the decisive acts of my life. I don't know if I will always have India in my thoughts, but I know that I will have India gnawing my liver.

It was in Kabul some months later that I began to be tired and weak. Driving south I became steadily more indolent. When we came north to Balkh that year I was thin and tired. Always tired. Began to become metaphysical. Had thoughts of intestines and death and life. Approaching the Pamirs I succumbed. Had to go back to Faizabad, where I was a vomiting, spineless thing.

Gun managed to get me back to our small mud hut in Kabul. There were letters waiting for us there. The magazines wanted articles. My publisher had written a nice letter reminding me that he had given me an advance for a book to be printed in the fall of 1958. It was now the fall of 1959, he said, and he still had not received any manuscript. We were very poor.

But I was floating in a void. My lassitude was not merely physical and mental, it had changed even my outlook. Of course I went regularly to the French library, read and made excerpts, was still functioning. But the amoebas gnawing my liver made me spiritual. The small earthquakes rolled by like thunder under the mountains, the rains came and the mud roof was falling over us. I lay in my sleeping bag, had taken a plastic sheet to cover myself, looked at the drops falling from the roof and said to Gun:

—The rains come, the mud dissolves. It is only natural. Here in this valley where we now live more than a hundred generations have seen their roofs dissolve.

—Get up, said Gun. Mend the roof.

I crept further into the cosy warmth of my sleeping bag under the plastic sheet shielding me from the wet.

—In my home province there is a stone standing in the memory of Harald who fell with Ingvar on the shores of the Caspian nine hundred years ago. It says:

Their foru drengila
fiarri at gulli
auk austarla
aerni gav
dou sunnarla
i saerklandi

—I don't understand you, Gun said.

—It is quite simple. A good verse. "They fared manly/ Far for gold/And eastwards/Fed the eagles/Died south-

wards/In Särkland." This is on the outskirts of Särkland,
you know. Do you think anybody will raise a stone for me?
—You are quite mad, said Gun.

And it was very strange. I was turning inwards like a
larva inside the cocoon of my sleeping bag. I had stopped
eating and when I was awake I thought about vague sub-
jects like Destiny and Man and Fate and Existence (all
with capitalization). Gun didn't like it. She started pack-
ing. Filled the car, dragged me out of my sleeping bag
saying:

—I'm not going to let you turn into an imago yet.

She drove us to Delhi, had me go to a doctor. We rented
the lower floor of a house in Defence Colony and I spent
four months in bed getting the amoebas under control.

The experience has led me to suspect that a large part
of that Asia, the one of soul and inwardness, that Europeans have such high regard for, is just the psychological
expression of physiological changes due to protozoans
eating the intestines.

If so, then at least the Europeans have done their best
to increase the soulfulness of the lesser races.

I woke up just after three o'clock in the morning. I found
myself speaking French. It was in the effort to word my
thoughts in a simple but at the same time classical and
clean French that I woke up. I sweated. Just as I opened
my eyes I heard my voice die out.

The curtains were pulled back. The moon was up and
there was a wide ribbon of moonlight passing over my
face. I turned away to get out of the light; on the white
wall above my pillow the moon had painted the window
sash into a cross of Lorraine. I got out of my bed and
walked to the window. The floor was cold. As I was getting
up my dog raised its head. Looked at me.

Beyond the glass the snowscape, the black forest, the

road. All clearly lighted and still. There was much light but no colour; a winter landscape in black and white. As a text in a trick movie I saw the thought shape itself, letter by letter, on the road in the lower edge of the picture: "The moonlit landscape has a graphic character; that, though, is due to the construction of the human eye, not to the spectrum of moonlight. A better eye would see colour in a moonlit landscape. That makes the difference between the floodlight of reality as compared to the theatrical effects." The thought stood out sharply against the snow. Then it passed and I listened towards the house; the deep cold was creaking in the wooden frame of the house. I had been talking to A. As I now looked towards the snow I found that I thought:

—And why speak French to A? A language she does not understand and I barely can work with. Would it not have been better to talk one of my languages? I might express myself in English; had I spoken Swedish she might also have understood.

The words sang clearly to me and I remembered at the same time that I had not spoken to her in second person singular. I had said *vous*. We had been walking down a dark street in the sixteenth arrondissement. All the shades were closed and all the blinds were down. The windows were dead. She had been wearing a silver-grey raincoat. It drizzled. She was a full head shorter than I. Listening to her footsteps. The drops of rain on her coat. Her hair. She had put her hand in mine and in the foreign language I had tried and groped to reach an honest declaration of love. She had turned her face towards me and I had looked into her eyes and talked very fast, time was short. All the time I had been stumbling over the French words.

There was a cold draught from the window and the forest rested darkly beyond the road. The dog had come up beside me. Stood up with its forepaws on the windowsill looking out into the night. I stroked its head and the long ears twitched under my hand. I felt a deep disquiet. It now worded itself as P's voice a couple of months ago:

—*Es ist später als du glaubst.*

The words turned around, reappeared in English, changing:

—It is later than you know, much later, too late.

Then more silently in Swedish:

—*Senare än du hoppats.*

And now I was quite awake and also remembered that A was already one year dead. The house was all silent. Not even the woodwork creaked. Gun seemed to sleep silently and I stood with my hand on the dog's head without being able to hear her breathe. I could clearly see the tracks of the fox. The marks led directly to the trash can. The fox was hungry. I had heard it sing earlier in the night. I turned around. In walking towards my bed I could see my shadow passing out of the moonlit ribbon and the cross of Lorraine once more sketched itself on the white wall.

The dream now returned. It rose to the surface in pieces and floes. Swirling. (The glistening greenish expanse of ice. The black icebreaker passing. The floes cutting back up to the surface. Turning.) The fragments formed a pattern, a sequence, a dream story. But when I organized them into this pattern I was well aware that this shaping of the dream was not that dream which had occurred as flashes and foreshortenings during sleep. This did not matter. I know that it is in the act of collecting the visual images, the verbal combinations, the fragments, that one simultaneously creates the dream story and the totality of the dream. The dream is composed and created only in the act of remembering. Thus one does not remember but shapes. But as long as the dreamer and the rememberer are—and must be—the same individual, this does not make any difference.

With an increasing sense of disquiet I staged the dream. The story began with the words:

—This night I dreamt about A but on waking up I realized that she was dead.

Later on I struck out those words. They were unnecessary.

I don't want to mislead. Therefore I ought to point out that I never had an affair with A. I never have tried. Had tried sounds better; she is dead.

Not because I didn't find her attractive. She was pretty and almost beautiful. She was young and had large eyes with which she admired. When I saw her for the first time and took her hand—she had warm hands but didn't take your hand, she put forth her hand to be taken—I, of course, thought that I would like to go to bed with her. So one thinks and so one reacts in general to women. But in that same moment I could also see the consequences. In the short moment I held her hand I had freedom of choice. I could hold on to her hand, look into her eyes and go straight ahead. I knew what would happen. I knew how such relations are enacted. I was not prepared to pay the price. I am not prepared to pay the price. Instead I draw my hand back, laugh and say:

—Hello.

So I am very moral. I base this morality on consciousness of freedom of choice. The life I want to live—the lack of fetters, the writing, Gun, much else—demands that I keep my motives and my actions in order. But I don't allow myself to suppress that experience of possibilities that certain women—far from all—give me when I meet them. Did I suppress that experience, then my life would become fettered, the freedom of choice would be gone. Thus unaccountable. Then I could suddenly act as I have seen so many act; tumble away in a spontaneous experience that is only conditioning; reflex and inhibition in acute conflict.

Insight gives me freedom; my morality is the choice of reason.

When the dream begins I am aware that there has been a prelude. A murder—and I am not the guilty one. A flight —during which I have probably sought an alibi for redress. A trial—so completely obscure that I only remember the word "trial." An execution—from which I have escaped. A new flight—and during this flight the dream starts.

I go up the stairs. Linoleum-covered steps with iron-shod corners. There is a pattern in the linoleum but it has worn down and out. Geometrical pattern, arabesque, it can still be seen in the corners near the wall. I open the double doors. They open in front of me and I enter the editorial office. Now in writing this I try to recall where I have seen this editorial office before. I can't. The picture is very clear and I know the rooms well. The room I am looking into has an atmosphere which reminds me of the first paper I worked on, *Värmlands Folkblad*. That was twenty years ago. I worked the night shift. Smell of stale beer. But I don't know from where this picture has been taken. All the association lines have been cut and all I find myself saying is, "The room has become larger but is also seen as in a mirror. Darkly."

No, just now when I rewrite the draft I am able to locate the picture. The circumstantial way in which I described the linoleum made me depressed and I quit writing. Lying on my couch reading Tucholsky and waiting to get in the mood for working, I see the curtain

go up. It was in Gothenburg in the summer of 1945. It was in July. On the nineteenth I had become eighteen. I had no money. I wrote out a subscription list on my office typewriter, "For the destitute." I went knocking on the doors, collecting. At this double door they gave me three crowns. It was a house in Nordenskjöld Street. Afterwards I felt ashamed. My friend Dag said:
—But this is becoming criminal.

I enter the office. In the dream I never say the name of the newspaper. I see the teleprinter compartment to the right. On that wall there are three doors. On a peg beside the first door hangs a black overcoat. To the left of me some people are sitting at their desks. They are blurred, as if they moved when the picture was taken. I am short of breath, tired, uneasy. Telephones ring. Straight ahead but far away is a huge desk. There are three persons sitting there. In the middle sits the subeditor. His chair is higher than the others.

Not until a moment after I have reached them do they look up from the desk and see me. My raincoat is wet, it is also torn on the left-hand side. It is the one I used in Belgrade 1948; the one that was heavy enough to be used as a ground sheet. I have my Swiss marching boots on. I see my tracks, they are clay-wet and follow me from the door. As the three at the table look up from their papers the whole room becomes all quiet.

(Now follows a long sequence. Sharp dialogue. Thrilling. It is bad. They discuss the murder I am said to have committed. They show me pictures of this. I point out that they have been lifted bodily from Söderman and O'Connel, *Modern Criminal Investigation.* I try to prove—what I feel is true—that everything is just construction, everything they say can be construed in a different manner. I have fled. Whether I am guilty or not is for the authorities to decide. I ought to be handed over to them. I walk towards the door. I only give an account of this long story. I find it embarrassingly badly done. After all, I would like to keep at least a minimum standard even in my dreams.)

I walk out of the office and the doors shut behind me. Three girls are sitting behind the reception desk. In the middle sits A. I lean my elbows on the counter and talk to her. Then she gets up from her chair and takes my hand. I talk very fast. She is leaving her place, saying nothing to the other girls that I now see in profile as they have turned towards their large typewriters. The floor separating me from the girls is a tile floor. The pattern is simple and large. A walks up to me over this floor and then follows me out into the night. I can see us walking out through the huge revolving doors. As I—through the ever more slowly revolving doors—see us two passing out onto the street, I feel how the autumn wind hits us when we step on the pavement. It rains.

I am very happy. I look at her. Her eyes are wide open. We stand on a street in the sixteenth arrondissement. Then I become aware of listening for footsteps in the darkness around us and in an anxiety-driven insight that my life is over and all doors are shut (I see a long corridor where doors are closing on either side like rows of falling domino pieces) I try to explain to her how much I love her and how much she means to me. I wake up talking French and wonder why I have not chosen to talk a language she can understand before I remember that A has been dead for nearly a year, that I never loved her, that she was of no importance to me as long as she was alive, and that she didn't even look like the A of my dream.

With the memory of waking up, I break off the dream. While going through the dream I had sat up in bed. Now I feel a sudden irritation and at the same time I notice that it is very cold. I once more get out of bed, put my slippers on and step along down the stairs. I don't walk, I step; irritated. In the middle of the staircase I stop, draw the curtains back and look at the outside thermometer. It is fifteen degrees centigrade below zero. I continue and walk through the library and study down into the basement. I switch on the light in the boiler room and check the boiler. Everything seems to be working normally. When I walk up the staircase from the basement and come out into the study I sense how the moonlight freezes the house. The rooms rest in a cold light, the books are shivering in their shelves and the disorderly paper piles cast shadow and darkness over the table top. I look at the indoor thermometer. Twenty-two degrees centigrade above zero. I am cold. The whole time the dog is walking behind me. He is sleepy, stretches. He yawns all the time. I go to bed again and pull the large Afghan sheepskin fell (the yellow one with the silver embroidery I bought in Kabul when I was there last two years ago) over me, wind it around my body. The dog lies down at the bottom of the bed. I rest my footsoles against his belly. It is warm.

I wait for the night to turn into early morning. The clock is pushing the time ahead beside my head. I am waiting for it to free me from the night. It is still winter and when I sit at my desk in the mornings after having coffee I can see the landscape getting lighter already at six thirty. The winter dawn comes grey over the snow, the forests and the ice-bound lake. Last summer I let down the sunblinds in my study. As yet I have not bothered to let them up. But I can look out. If somebody lies with a field glass at the forest's edge on the other side of the lake he can't look in. At regular intervals I feel this to be a good joke. In between I explain to myself that this is practical because it makes it unnecessary for me to wash the seven large windows in my study. Rationality and rationalization.

Now in my bed—the dog sleeping—I think about yesterday's work. Life is a continuous process of reorientation;
sometimes you move so far that all the perspectives you
once saw have been twisted out of all proportion and have
lost all connection with the new reality surrounding you.
The movement in space—the geographical journeys—of
mine since 1958 by-and-by forced me to new intellectual
co-ordinates.

Doesn't this all sound beautiful? It seems so sincere
and so honest that I now—some months later—feel
nausea when reading it. I mistrust these words so much
that when reading them aloud I begin to cough until I
turn deep red in the face and vomit. Still, I can't actually catch myself in lies. It is true even though it sounds
true.

Asia changed my perspectives. Warped them, some
critics say. I had known a great deal about Asia before we
arrived there. What an educated European is supposed to
know. It was not ignorance; it was a European perspective.
This had to be corrected. The West. An appendix to
Eurasia. Our "Western culture" the vermiform appendix
to the larger cultures. And the European perspective the
vermiformocentric idea. I am not joking. It is not only a
question of reading the parallel traditions, the Arabic, the
Chinese. It is also the painful change of perspectives. In
our schools and at our universities the teachers and the
professors have been salaried to falsify history. They do it.
They do it willingly.

This does not mean that I became a mystic. The mysticism of the East is accepted. As drugs are accepted. Table
dances are accepted. The suburbanites of the West become
mystics or let tables dance or take drugs and it is all the
same. The mysticism of the East is just amoebic dysentery.
One or the other. It makes no difference. Soulfulness.

The teachers of the West. The *Hirnverherer*, as Brecht said. The justificators of every robbery, every plunder. The falsifiers. Suddenly anger hammering at my temples. Dry throat. If the learned men had but one neck . . .

I laugh. This I mean. I can't write it. My words won't reach anyone. They are immune. I could as well talk to a white man in the "West" about the equality of Man.

To change the perspectives is to change one's ideas. In India I had found that there were two roads open to me. To keep my ideas and once and for all know that they in reality—Asian reality—carried the meaning of white supremacy, colonialism, imperialism and war. They were after all the same European values that all these experts and diplomats and businessmen from the Western countries (from Vladivostok over Berlin, Paris, London, New York to Los Angeles) at suitable moments used as cover for their activities. If I refused to accept this consequence . . . then I had to acquire new perspectives suited to a larger reality. This meant reading. But as the days have too few hours and as I—as everybody else—must have beer and potatoes (or preferably whisky and meat) to keep alive, I sat through the nights reading Ibn Khaldun, Chinese classics, Indian history. Not mainly for the sake of learning—even though it is always fun to read—but in order to remould myself; to break down my ethnocentric "Western" perspectives. To seek and destroy the ideologies, the thought patterns and the prejudices that our schools and newspapers, friends and employers fill us with in Europe. One can't only say intellectually that one does not take part. One has to change even one's basic outlook.

You can also break the ideologies by taking them seriously. This can be done in the following stages:

A) The platitude: Man (capital m) is created equal.

You can't hear a president speak, a prime minister talk without this phrase being used. All of them just love equality.

B) The reality: man is a decidedly unequalized beast. Few are rich and powerful. Many are hungry and oppressed.

Now it is up to you to decide. Let us say you are in Latin America. You can go to conferences and United Nations meetings and get good pay for saying that Man (capital m) is created equal. That never hurts any dividends. Or you can say that men (existing men) are treated like beasts.

If you take the first choice—then you follow the Western tradition by breaking its ideology. If you take the second choice, then you pick up your *ametralladora* and do something about the beastliness.

The dog looks at me. It is my dog. Whose dog am I? And where should I go with my machine gun? I fulfil a function in a society that I for good reasons consider insane. The function of writing.

While I sit in my bed and build words around *ametralladora* the truth is that I do no such thing. That I did later. Long after that night.

Turn back and rewrite!

Asia changed all my perspectives. I had known something about Asia, of course. What an educated European is supposed to know. That was not ignorance. But it was a European perspective. This had to be corrected. After I returned to Sweden I had in a planned fashion tried to read up on the parallel traditions, Arabian and Chinese. Consciously seek other perspectives on the development. It ought to be pointed out that this is not the same as becoming a mystic. Only changing the perspectives. As the days have too few hours and as I—like everybody else—

have to earn my living, I sat up during nights and read Ibn Khaldun, Chinese classics, Indian history. Not just for the sake of knowledge—even if it always is a pleasure to read—but in order to break down my ethnocentric European perspective in a planned fashion. Of course, the breaking down of this particularism is also the demand that this European intellectual tradition makes.

Drowsing, I was turning these thoughts over and over waiting for morning. I was utilizing a quotation from Needham's *Science and Civilisation in China*, Volume 3, page 196:

> The postface to the first part of the *Lü Shih Chhun Chhiu* itself then tells us that it was completed in −239. This was not the last time in history when a politically powerful but (even in its own opinion) relatively uncultured society would make great efforts to attract to itself the best of light and learning which existed elsewhere; examples could be found readily enough in Mongol Persia and later on the North American continent.

I like his style. The dry gibe. But more than that: if the conscious lack of culture (Timurids) formerly had led to a cultural development (Wei and Timuridian renaissance) could then the conscious lack of culture on "the North American continent" possibly have the same consequences now? Were the wars of the United States (and we all know what to think of them) more inhuman than those of the Mongols? About the Mongols could it be said what was said about Mussolini . . . the roads functioned?

When rewriting this I became disturbed. Something was wrong. I saw no reason why I had written these sentences. The idea was puerile. (Not Needham's, but

mine.) As a statement of fact—yes. (Brain-drain.) As
an evaluation—no. I went down to my library and took
out the volume. On the front flyleaf I had written:
"p. 196 uncultured societies
p. 358 learning and dying (see Ssu-ma Ch'ien)
p. 522 when was Europe discovered?"
The whole day before I dreamt about A had been
spent reading Needham, Volume 3. Those notes had
been written then. I had been sleepily speculating about
"the North American continent" and the cultural value
of a conscious lack of culture, but a rather different—
and much more important—problem had occupied me
during the day; had influenced the staging of my dream.
"P. 358 learning and dying (see Ssu-ma Ch'ien)": the
quotation I had underlined was one that Needham had
translated from Huan Than (−40 to +30):

> Yang Hsiung was devoted to astronomy and used to
> discuss it with the officials. . . . He made an armillary
> sphere himself. An old artisan once said to him:
> "When I was young I was able to make such things
> following the method of divisions (graduations) to
> scale . . . without really understanding their mean-
> ing. But afterwards I understood more and more.
> Now I am seventy years old, and feel that I am only
> just beginning to understand it all, and yet soon I
> must die. I have a son also, who likes to learn how to
> make these instruments; he will repeat the years of
> my experience, and some day I suppose he in his turn
> will understand, but by that time he too will be ready
> to die." How sad, and at the same time how comical,
> were his words!

There was something very strange in the way I had
speculated about the Timurids and the United States.
I had mentioned Ibn Khaldun: "Little effort is being

made to get at the truth. The critical eye, as a rule, is not sharp. Errors and unfounded assumptions are closely allied and familiar elements in historical information. . . . It takes critical insight to sort out the hidden truth, takes knowledge to lay truth bare and polish it so that critical insight may be applied to it." But the reference to Ssu-ma Ch'ien makes it understandable why I—in the waking interlude of my dream with A—chose to turn away from the old artisan, turn away from Ibn Khaldun.

That Arab scholar, who was born in Tunis in 1332 and who travelled and studied all over the civilized world—Africa, Spain, western Asia—and died in Cairo in 1406, was the first "modern" historian. Had I really been working with the problem of shifting my perspectives, then I of course should have been trying to get his work into focus. How could he be so many centuries ahead of the European barbarians? And why is he never read in our schools, unknown to the "reading public" in Europe and only a concern of the "specialists"?

For my personal problems, though, the anecdote of the old artisan was more relevant. That can be seen on the flyleaf. The pressure of the pencil is harder in that annotation than in the one before or the one after. But it was too relevant.

Ssu-ma Ch'ien was Great Astrologer or Grand Historian (or keeper of records) to the great Emperor Wu of the former Han dynasty. He wrote the first systematic—scientific you might say—history of the world (as seen from the civilized centre, of course) in China. Not the first history. But the first and the greatest critical systematization. His official post was low; far below the high-sounding title. But he had access to the records and the reports of the empire and he knew that what he was doing was of importance for unborn generations. He was founding a tradition.

Emperor Wu was smashing the nobility, securing the south, unifying the country, conquering the west, rewriting the codes and striving to establish the Chinese Peace over the known world. When in −99 a young captain by the name of Li Ling was defeated by the Huns in the eastern Tien Shan and only four hundred out of the five thousand who had marched out were able to return, the Emperor Wu was provoked to wrath. The defeat was small. The defeat mattered little to the empire; but the literati of the court all condemned Li Ling.

Ssu-ma Ch'ien knew Li Ling but slightly. But he spoke in the council to Emperor Wu about Li Ling's merits. Li Ling had been near victory, but had not been supported. He said that few generals in the past had fought as well as Li Ling.

But the commanding general had been Li Kuang-li. He had failed. Thus what Ssu-ma Ch'ien said was a criticism of his actions. The sister of General Li Kuang-li was Lady Li. At this time she was the favorite of Emperor Wu. Consequently Ssu-ma Ch'ien was ordered by the emperor to be handed over to the judges for deceiving the Throne.

There were two ways of escape for Ssu-ma Ch'ien. He could buy himself free. But his friends deserted him and he himself was poor. He could also commit suicide. He should commit suicide. His obligation to his tradition, to his family, to his social standing was clear. The honourable man does not appear before the judges.

Ssu-ma Ch'ien did not commit suicide. He was condemned. He was whipped. He was castrated. And he continued living as a shamed man, a mutilated man, a man without honour. In a letter to a friend, Jen Shao-ch'ing, who was in jail and who would be executed, Ssu-ma Ch'ien gave his reasons.

If even the lowest slave and scullion maid can bear to commit suicide, why should not one like myself be able to do what has to be done? But the reason I have not refused to bear these ills and have continued to live, dwelling in vileness and disgrace without taking my leave, is that I grieve that I have things in my heart which I have not been able to express fully, and I am shamed to think that after I am gone my writings will not be known to posterity. . . . I have gathered up and brought together the old traditions of the world which were scattered and lost. I have examined the deeds and events of the past and investigated the principles behind their success and failure, their rise and decay, in one hundred and thirty chapters. I wished to examine into all that concerns heaven and man, to penetrate the changes of the past and present. . . . But before I had finished my rough manuscript, I met with this calamity. It is because I regretted that it had not been completed that I submitted to the extreme penalty without rancor. When I have truly completed this work, I shall deposit it in the Famous Mountain. If it may be handed down to men who will appreciate it, and penetrate to the villages and great cities, then though I should suffer a thousand mutilations, what regret should I have? . . . Though a hundred generations pass, my defilement will only become greater. This is the thought that wrenches my bowels nine times each day. Sitting at home, I am befuddled as though I had lost something. I go out, and then realize that I do not know where I am going. Each time I think of this shame, the sweat pours from my back and soaks my robe. I am now no more than a servant in the harem. . . . Therefore I follow along with the vulgar, floating and sinking,

bobbing up and down with the times, sharing their
delusion and madness. . . . Only after the day of death
shall right and wrong at last be determined. *

Semiconsciously I preferred not to state the problem
of the intellectual in those terms. With full consciousness I did; unconsciously I feared; but drowsing I tried
to walk down a road that would be an escape but not a
betrayal. You will see whether I succeeded.

Of course I realize that this description can be misunderstood. It can be read as if this nighttime work with Ibn
Khaldun and Needham, my speculations about the cultural value of lack of a culture, about the Europeocentric
world-view and the necessary new co-ordinates, was a private defence; a flight and a series of rationalizations. Intellectualism being used as protection against menacing
emotional experiences. I will come back to the question of
intellectualism and emotions; the double insight.

But I cannot see reasoning as "flight" or "defence." The
intellectual work is not rationalization but rationality, reason. The tension you can feel between the clear and
translucent intellectuality and the primal, the Panic emotion, is a fruitful tension. It drives you forward. It is the
flight into emotional experiences, into "immediateness"
that is a defence against the intensity of emotions. Only
through a direct awareness and an intellectual insight that
makes the flow of events and the experiences of the self
into a sequence of explainable and inevitable phenomena,
can one dare let the emotions through. I will come back
to this.

Once more I want to point out that I am not truthful.
I censor. I strike out. Displace. Foreshorten. Condense. I
do this in the name of truthfulness. (And—I hope—in its

* Burton Watson, *Ssu-Ma Chi'en: Grand Historian of China* (New York, Columbia
University Press, 1958), pp. 65–67.

interest.) Neither do I care to analyze in detail that chain of causation that determined both the dream and the discussion about Needham.

I wrote these words in order to give myself reasons for striking out a dream sequence connected with certain personal sexual experiences. I did not strike it out because of prudishness; we are all brothers under the skin. Our masturbatory phantasies are also remarkably stereotyped —as can be easily seen if one reads pornography. I had struck it out because the sequence involved a third person. One whom I know not to like being described. Not even in the form of a dream. For myself I don't have (as far as I know) any sense of shame. But I have found that others have. She would—like Victoria—have conveyed to me that she was not amused.

But now I see that there was also quite another link between the dream and Needham that I did strike out. One that was not a dream. I had utilized the erotic censorship to censor a more important discussion. (Which is quite normal and social.)

When I lay awake that moonlit night and phrased sentences about the culture—or the strange lack of culture —of the United States it is once more 1940 and we walk Riverside Drive north. I and Nelson and Theobald. The sun is shining. A tug goes up the river. There is a slight haze in the air. Nelson talks about China. He had grown up there, his father was a missionary.

—Father cried when Wang Ching-wei joined the Japanese. He had been the best of the lot and father knew him well.

I see it very clearly. It is near Grant's tomb. We are now under the drive. High above us the ironwork, rusty, the rumbling sound of the heavy traffic. We climb. We stand on the highest girder. It is covered with a deep layer of grime and black, sticky dirt. Theobald's father is a social-

ist. (I believe that he was a German-Jewish emigree.)
We talk about the war. Our teacher, Mr. F, has spoken to
us about the First World War.

—Don't believe what you read. My generation did. It
was dirt and death, and all just because the European
powers had their intrigues and Morgan had invested heavily in an Entente victory. Ordinary American boys like you
here got killed just for the sake of high finance and secret
diplomacy. I have seen it.

Then R, whose father was a banker and knew the President (it was said), leaned towards me and said:

—Not just because of Morgan. We know what the Germans are like.

In the Second World War both Theobald and Nelson
are killed. But then, in the spring of 1940, we balance
high up on a grimy girder and speak about the occupation
of Denmark by the Germans.

There is a policeman standing on the street. I see his
cap. There are old newspapers and orange peels in the
gutter beside him. Just beside us hangs a platform under
the road. Probably they use it for inspection purposes.
The platform is so far from the girder that you can't touch
it even with your fingertips. Not just by stretching out
your hand. You can't even let yourself fall towards it, get
a grip on the rim and then heave up on it. You have to
stand back, tighten your muscles and then leap over to it.
The girder shakes and trembles from the heavy traffic
above our heads. The policeman has gone. There are some
children standing down there now. They look towards
us. They look up to us but laugh. Point their fingers. We
don't dare to jump, they say. They are now shouting up
towards us. A small girl in a red dress jumps up and down
on the pavement, she is very exited and says that we don't
dare.

The girders are red with rust and black with soot. On

the platform is our hiding place. There we are alone. There the gang meets. We used to sit there and let our legs swing free above the street, read comics, talk about girls—there is a wind blowing from the river. And far away the Palisades. It is very high above the street. I remember how we jump, take the leap from the girder to the inspection platform. The sucking fear coming up from the genitals as you leap. Not to dare, and then suddenly to find yourself already jumping because you have not dared not to dare.

On the platform the dirt is a deep layer of soot. Now we feel the traffic vibrating close to our heads. We have to bend our heads when we sit here. When we get home we will go to Nelson's place. He lives in the house next to mine. Otherwise somebody will ask me where I have been.

These memories are very distinct. The thoughts have leaped from A to Riverside Drive 1940. Doing so through Needham and the situation of culture on the "North American continent."

But for the first time in twenty-three years I suspect that this memory is spurious. I have told the story many times. (Told it in passing, not made a detailed study of it.) The first time I remember telling it is September 1940. Then I was just back in Sweden. The war was very near. Dag and I are standing under the Traneberg Bridge just at the barbed wire. The men at the anti-aircraft guns are smoking. They wave to us. I speak to Dag. Talk about New York and our hiding place. But the story can't possibly be true. The memory is a false one, a pseudo-memory. Theobald can't have been along. He lived on the other side of the river. It happened only once that we met after school. He always went straight home. The only time I met him outside of school hours was at Nelson's party. I was dressed up as a Chinese coolie. I had bought the dress in a small shop near Times Square. (I found a picture

from that party when I burned papers, letters and photos
when I came back to Sweden in 1963 and packed up my
stored belongings.)

Even this must be lies, though. I remember this photo.
It was taken in school. I was not dressed like a Chinese
coolie. I was dressed like a clown. I hated the picture.
I smiled an asinine smile in it. A fat boy smiling. And
as I write this—1967—I suddenly remember Nelson's
party. I was dressed like a Chinese, that is true. But the
shopkeeper had had his joke. It was a Chinese dress
all right, but a woman's dress. I remember how they
laughed. All the family laughed. Tears of laughter came
into their eyes. And I smiled and smiled and smiled.
God! I hated it. No wonder I construed other memories
when I wrote this three years ago.

And the role that Nelson plays in this story seems strange.
I don't even remember for sure if we went to the same class
or not. Or the same school. But we were neighbours. He
collected stamps. I once dropped a box of Chinese stamps
on Riverside Drive. They blew away. He was sorry, he
said. He liked his stamps. His sister had visited Sweden in
1937 (why?). No, Nelson was not one of the three who
climbed up towards that high girder.
   I read through what I have written. I am struck by the
ease with which I wrote off Theobald and Nelson as victims of the war. Were they? I wrote some letters to Nelson
in 1941 or 1942. I must have got some answer. Somewhere
I think I have heard or read that he fell in the war against
Japan. But I don't know. Lies in memory like moths in
clothes. If you wait long enough before you air them
there will be only doubt, dust and shreds when you open
the door.
   But—the big fights around 124th Street were real.

Though I can no longer remember who was on my side. If anyone. Shadows and dim faces. Voices. They took the same road home as I did. They were cowards, I thought. They did not stand up and fight when the gang tried to stop us. They fled. They said that one ought not to fight in the streets. So said the school psychologist. I belonged to a class that did not fight in the streets. That was what she thought.

—We do in Sweden, I said.

—But you are not in Sweden, she said. You hurt the reputation of the school. We must keep our reputation even though we are so close to the slums. You must always remember that you are a pupil of a fine school.

—If they leave me in peace I won't fight. If they don't leave me in peace I have to fight. Nobody has the right to spit in my face.

When I was going home that day the boys from the 124th Street stood in my way. They just stood there blocking me. I tried to go straight ahead but they stopped me. The others from my school turned around and took another way. My English was poor, it was during my first months in New York; I said in my bad English:

—If you don't step out of my way I spit you in the face.

The boy was large. He was taller than me. He understood me. But he thought I was joking. All of his gang laughed. They were whistling. Freckled faces. In the meantime I stood all still and gathered saliva and mucus in my mouth. When his big red face came eighteen inches from me I spat him between the eyes. It dripped down his cheeks. Then we fought. I had known that I should lose. They were many. I regained consciousness in a delicatessen store. The owner had dragged me in there. His wife gave me water. She was fat.

The school psychologist spoke to me again and again. She said that she would talk to my parents. I don't know if she did. She never understood that you have to keep your self-respect. And I despised her for that.

But after I had spat the gang leader between the eyes and his gang had beaten me senseless I never had any trouble on my way home from school. He greeted me when we passed. I understood him. He understood me. But the boys in my class never understood me. They laughed at me and R said:

—Only a Swede can be that stupid.

—But I won, didn't I? I said.

Still they could not understand.

That was not my last street fight. The last one was in 1947. It was the year I was going to be called into military service. We had been drinking at a hotel in the south of Sweden, in Urshult. There was a market there that day. People were fighting with bridles down at the horse fair. A man with black hair stood yelling in the middle of the market, just under the lamp, and swung the bridle round and round. I came out of the hotel. I was drunk. We were looking for our car. The car was to fetch us. I saw a couple of girls. I talked to them. Then we stood waiting. Out there on the gravel came a blond boy. He was shouting. He knocked down a man. He said he was going to kill anybody who came up. I had the girls beside me. I sniggered. I laughed at him. He asked me if I wanted to fight. I said that I never fought with small people. Midgets, you know. He struck me. I gave him a cigarette. Just as I was saying that I didn't fight with people like him, he rammed me straight in the face with the back of his head. As I had opened my mouth and was talking just then, my front teeth got stuck in his skull and broke. Then I got mad. We fought. I said that I was going to kill him. Kill him for real. The girls were there. When I got him down he smashed his head against the curbstone. He bled. I had my hands around his throat and said Now you die, brother. Then came the police. But he was a drunk sailor who had fought many times in this small village. I was a drunk journalist and the girls were witnesses that I had not wanted to fight and that I had tried to calm him. He said that I had laughed. He had cracked his skull in the fall but I had broken two teeth. The judge found him guilty. I never met the girls again. I visited him in the hospital. I didn't want him to misunderstand. I didn't want any money for my teeth. It was the judge's idea. I gave him the money back. He said: "It was a beautiful fight anyway." I have never seen him since. That was my last fight. I had laughed. The fault was mine.

The three boys walking north and passing Grant's tomb that spring morning of 1940 must have been I and two others. I don't know who. But I know, and know utterly and anxiously, that I have stood on top of this girder and felt the nausea of my leap towards the platform. I also know that I once did take that leap. I wonder if I was quite alone that time I did dare the leap. To see myself dare to.

But when we were playing in the attic sometime in autumn 1939 I slipped while running along a girder. I fell and hurt myself. Hands, feet, back. Spent three weeks in bed lying on my stomach. Listened to the Lone Ranger.

The only thing that remains of the story I have told for twenty-three years (told now and then) is the taste of iron, rusty iron under my palms as I climb upwards; everything else is lies. Lies and goddamned poetry. Fictions I have collected here and there in order to make myself believe the story.

It was the memory of this process that I struck out.
And it was when I reached this awareness of my own de-
ceitfulness and the lack of real sharpness in my insight
that I, with a loathful intensity, could make myself conscious that the nightly dream had not at all ended just by
me making a declaration of love to A who is now one year
dead.

The lack of truth goes one step further. Coming
back to New York in 1966 I spent three nights looking
for this girder, this bridge; it was in February and it
was cold. Gun complained. She didn't like walking these
streets up and down in search of childhood. She found
me ridiculous. What I never told her, though, was that
I could not find the place. It had no existence outside
of my memories. That far I did not trust even her. She
left New York believing I had really seen my childhood.
The only thing I saw was the house in which I had
lived. My school was torn down and my secret hiding
place had been so secret that it never even existed.

First some swiftly changing scenes. I am hardly able to
see more than a couple of faces (Breughel sketches) in a
mass of people; a stream of people gushing forth through
a narrow alley; then now and then an upturned face, suddenly flashed with light and set off against the moving
dark mass. Far away some shots. Wider street: heavy
trucks. Car burning. Trucks, tarpaulin-covered. Something
moving under the tarpaulin. Once more faces, this time
magnified, distorted (Bosch through a bad reading glass),
then eyes, only eyes. Afterwards dark.

The cell is dark. I am aware that it is built with huge,
roughly hewn stone blocks. It is too dark for me to see the
joints but when I grope with my paws I find that the walls
are damp. The stones arch above my head. I cannot reach

the arch. But I know that it is there. The march of boots in the passage. Heel-irons. See in the darkness boots kicking forth through the dark passage; as the heel-irons strike the stone floor, sparks shower the wall. Tramping sound and showers of sparks. Dark.

I am in a far larger cell now and the prison is a modern one. The bunks are turned up. It is daylight. Just in front of the door the sun has painted the grating on the floor. The door is open. When I look out through the doorway the gallows stands on the hill like a stage setting. Now the strong emotional engagement that characterized the beginning of the dream sequence fades out. I do not say, "This is only a dream." But everything has become just like my ordinary reality; decoration and theatre.

I seem to be saying, "In my thirtieth year I see you hanging there, blackened by the sun, and I have pity on you." But I am thirty-seven.

Two men in grey prison dress are sweeping the floor with long piassava brooms. They talk to each other. Certainly I can hear them. Their voices are very clear, but I don't listen to their words. They gesticulate. The picture sketched in light colours with clear and sharp outlines. I stand in the doorway of my cell and look at the picture. It is so decidedly a picture (l'art nouveau).

I do not recognize it. But if I look to my right I see that I stand in a prison by Piranesi. As I think this (and at the same time listen to the recording of a discussion about Escher and his staircase pictures that Gun and I had last autumn in Paris) I am reached by the noises of an interrogation that apparently is being held in another part of the prison.

—Exactly what do you mean; were the children thrown in alive or were they killed in some way before being cremated?

—Well, in the graves the children were thrown in alive.

One could hear their screams everywhere in the camp. That was of course very annoying. It is a surprising amount of sound that can be produced by such a small body. The technical staff of the gas chambers at that time worked around the clock and we had to take the limited capacity of the equipment into account. Therefore we began putting the children into the oven without gassing them first. That lessened the noise level. This of course saved both material and working time but was very inconvenient. They kicked as they were thrown in. One of us got bitten. But orders were orders.

Now the yard around the gallows is very much 1910 and Carl Larsson. Small Dalecarlian girls (blond) in the national dress of my village walk around in the fat green grass collecting spring flowers for a wreath, for a garland. I stand on the balcony and say:

—Today we may celebrate the hundredth anniversary of the Swedish freedom from hanging. This is the fifth freedom.

Once more faces, a stream of faces. I am sitting in an ordinary cell in a Swedish police station (Växjö, September 1947). The blanket I have wound around my body stinks of sour old spew. Stiff with dirt. The lamp shines in my face. I can't even break it. There is an iron net protecting the lamp. My buddy, my big, stupid, friendly buddy, is getting it. When I stand on tiptoe and look out through the small cell window I can see him being hanged. It is very festive. Drums and flags and cheers. He is being led up the wooden steps. He resists. He seems to scream. I see his mouth wide open and he tries to move his arms. I am possibly very scared. He is being brought to the gallows by two Swedish policemen in their summer uniforms. (Ice-cream vendors, balloons, general gaiety.)

Then all doors spring open and I see me running. I

run through the prison and it is all empty. I wonder why all doors now spring open.

Still picture: Rowlandson. "Visiting an old friend." The two riders in front of the hanged man. The corpse mouldering on the gallows. The gaping mouths of the visitors.

I stand in front of the picture, turn aside and say:

—The leap from a bloody reality to a late romantic picaresque takes but a short time. Thus, Jan Potocki's "Manuscrit trouvé à Saragosse." The incessant repetition of the hanging sequence becomes a thrilling entertainment. You ought to remember, though, that Rowlandson was five years older than Potocki. But Potocki shot himself in Uladowka twelve years before Rowlandson died and Rowlandson died exactly one hundred years before you were born. The motif of the hanged man and his friend during this time develops rapidly. It changes with a recklessly neckbreaking speed. In your delights over Potocki and his polemics against the general reaction you ought to remember that it took one hundred and forty-eight years before his manuscript was published for the first time in its entirety. And then in German. And then —1963—the Holy Alliance was but a memory and the polemics against Chateaubriand had lost their meaning as had Le Génie du christianisme (Mutter) and he was only known as the name of a piece of meat on the menu. Thus the hanging now becomes only a picaresque.

This long monologue was delivered with great seriousness. While delivering it I saw it accompanied (as in a musical score) with footnotes. Footnote-studded delivery.

Then, once more, I run. I pass a cross-corridor. A wide band of light runs over the floor. It comes from a small room on the left. A sits bound to a chair. She is being garrotted. I see her eyes.

—Goya, I think.

But now the dream ends in a last picture of doors being flung open and the street full of people.

In a confused awakening I say:

—A is dead. She is dead.

And I remember that during the war, when I was fifteen years old, in 1942, I found that one of my friends looked at Goya's "Carretadas al cementerio" as pornography. He used to masturbate in front of that etching. The girl was so beautiful, he thought.

Not so innocuous then the discussion on Needham and the Wei dynasty.

The work with this manuscript has been slow. I have been in pain. It is now a month since I last answered letters. The papers collect on my desk. The only thing I have been able to produce is a couple of articles. It is already spring. Patches of snow on bare ground. I took a long walk with my dog this morning. I felt the smell of soil, the birches already have a violet haze around them. Spring.

Pain, physical pain, has interesting consequences. One has to concentrate. The words become heavy to carry. And there is a feeling of lacking time. In the night, before I go to sleep, I have been lying awake in bed thinking about a historical novel. Of course I intend to describe my own time. One where the rockets crouch in their cement caverns ready to leap. It is a strange situation to belong to a dying culture in a doomed world. But as it is nearly impossible to make reality conscious to the readers I wanted to dress the consciousness in historical dress.

I assume that the reader has conditioned reflexes that defend him from a direct attempt to give him insight into his situation. But one could creep up on him; find a field where he has not been prepared. No brainwashing can ever be complete, so one ought to be able to find the weak link in his defenses. Then a short sharp thrust of reason, followed up by getting him to see himself from outside for just a moment. Then maybe his consciousness can take over and make a human being out of him before the insane normality of our Western culture once more mechanizes him. I found myself thinking this. But that is too rationalistic. I have no such belief in literature except when I am made lightheaded by alcohol or sleepiness. In fact the subject of the novel interested me even if that subject was historical and was doom and death. Because just that subject was a doom which we had survived by many hundreds of years. And sometimes I hope that at least some people—somewhere—will survive the next fifty years and tell of us. Though I often find this very doubtful.

So I have been awake at nights seeing a novel in front of me. A novel wide like a river, epic, tragic (heroic). Sentences clear and direct. Characters hewn in blocks. The fall of the Northman culture in Greenland. A New York friend of mine, hearing about this, said, "Of all the cultures this seems the most alien and the most meaningless." My point being of course that it was not in the least an "alien culture" from our Western point of view—but it was meaningless. Of the founding we know. The United States now and then even gives out commemorative stamps about the westbound Vikings. *That skal at minnum manna/ medhan menn lifa.* "That shall men remember/ whilst men live." But I was to tell the rest of the story. The saga of the dead.

The Northerners came as farmers and cattle breeders to the Arctic. Theirs was an abortive colonization, doomed from the very beginning. It became a long and vicious dying out. The Eskimos were what they called themselves, Innuit, men; reasonable, human. The Eskimos were adjusted. But the Northerners came with their long ships

and their Scandinavian culture. The wait for ships from
Europe. The political revolutions in northern Europe that
destroyed the survival chances of the faraway settlement
by changing the pattern of trade. Degeneration and
death. I would like to work with it. People. Years. Landscape. The slanting light. Have spoken to Gun about
moving to Greenland for a year, but she does not want to.
It will take time to convince her. I have placed books on
Greenland in different strategic positions in the house but
she collects them, gives them to me and says:

—Greenland does not interest me.

Slowly I prepare for the journey to Greenland. And I
wonder what I will eventually write. But I also sense that
this planning for Greenland is just another attempt to flee.
The pain turns me inward. Maybe it helps give me a certain limited honesty. Pain creating consciousness. Danger,
the ease with which you then slide into mysticism, meta-
physics.

Then it is also possible that my experience of intense
and incessant pain so changes my view of the surrounding
world that the subject, which is in itself tragic—the destruction of the Northmen in Greenland—would become
melodramatic. The inevitability becoming sentiment.
What did the girl sing? And who tried to wave to the
last ship? The ship that never entered the port because
the wind was bad. That hand waving, that running figure
was the last anybody (from a surviving culture) saw of
the Northmen in Greenland. The things I see at night have
become too romantic. Falling turf roofs, deformed skele-
tons. The last men in the last hut. Shivering. Death and
emptiness. Not even they were conscious of their fate.
Even they might have believed. (Here I can put in religion. They prayed. Or at least they had a bishop for some
time. But I don't like religions. Having gods is such a
cowardly flight from reality.) Death by stupidity. The

Northmen were destroyed as they sought a freedom outside the objective reality (nature, the climate, their
level of technology). Freedom leading to future when it
follows objective reality—Eskimos. Every morning I make
notes in a small black book: "But if obj. real. itself—fate
—leads to death & destr. where then the diff. poss. freedom?"

On proofreading:
What is stated above becomes shorthand and com-
pressed. Must put it straight. The perspectives on the
Greenland book are the perspectives on our time.

When Eirik the Red took land westward he had first
landed under the glacier Bluesark. He later settled
southward at Eiriksfjord. But as he, after having spent
three winters in the new land, returned to Iceland, he
named his newfound land Greenland. With that name
it was easier to get settlers there.

This—tactically necessary (and as tactic by his contemporaries in his culture as slyly accepted)—gap between reality and illusion the settlers could never bridge.

They sought their freedom in the illusion Greenland. The dead from the Middle Ages lie in their graves
dressed in the fashions of their times; fashions from
Paris and the Burgundian court. Not the reasonable
dress, the rational dress, the dress for Bluesark and
Whitesark.

First stage: the tragedy they experienced. The isolated. Those who had been cut off. Those who were
ridden by the dim consciousness that they were dying
out and that they were driven (like cattle) to destruction by forces they could not master. The tragedy of
fatefulness.

Second stage: the clarification that fate was not fate
but lack of insight and consciousness. Their culture was

unreasonable. Already in the naming of Greenland lay hidden the destruction. The historical tragedy. Gruesome because the responsibility has been changed from fate to human activity.

Finally:—as the last step—demasking also the historical tragedy. Here is the difficulty. The possibility of freedom. In every now was waiting the possibility of freedom. The freedom of blubber, the freedom of the igloo, the freedom of necessity. No fate decided for them. They thought wrong, they decided wrong and they died for it. The wages of stupidity are death. There's the weak link. (Where are your descendants, Eirik? What happened to your seed? What never dies, Eirik? The doom of a dead man.)

The inevitability of this process. The deep and awful human tragedy. The eyes. The hands. The last saga said. The last man who hoped. (Behind this—the knowledge that the hope always could be fulfilled. That their future always was bright. That freedom was theirs.)

Epic form. No reasoning. Dirge for the heroes of yesteryear. But where the tragic is not fate but the everlasting freedom of choice; the culturally conditioned behaviour. Heroics where heroism is denied and turned into its counterpart without losing its quality of deep human suffering. Omniscient author (omniscient because born later), thus omniscient reader. The figures moving as in a large ball of glass.

It will take many years of work. But just because what has been has been and thereby is a part of the rigid and unalterable past, it might give the reader (with the slowly moving epic form) the possibility of freedom for the future.

There must be a future some months or some years ahead when I can breathe freely. Breathe calmly and rhythmically without pain, work smoothly and follow the epical flow. But today I am better. I have started to clear the piles of paper. I even answer letters. Am sitting at my desk the whole day.

Pain as creating consciousness. A dangerous theory. But justified. Becomes dangerous only when the pain is being brought in as a necessary step in the process of making conscious. Pain as a positive experience *for others.* The torturer's philosophy. Inquisition.

In former years we used to tell a funny story about S.

While proofreading:
I went to the bookshop when I had written the former chapter, I took the *Occult Diary* by Strindberg. It had just been published (though even now in an "edited" version). To the discussion on pain and consciousness. Strindberg describes how Harriet Bosse is "seeking" him. Organic sensations. (The Swedish critics surprise me. They wrote about the *Occult Diary* as if it were a diary, as if they got "an insight" into the "hidden personality" of Strindberg. But the *Diary* was written to be published. Strindberg was a writer. He never even wrote a love letter without having publication in mind. The story about the occult marriage seems quite normal to me, though made into "literature." Have the reviewers really never been in love, longed—with shame and hatred—for a certain woman, dreamt and masturbated? But possibly Swedish critics don't masturbate.)

Strindberg prays to God for a "thorn in the flesh." He feels the "seeking" of Harriet Bosse to be more and more of a pain. The next to the last entry in the published diary reads: "Days of horror! So horrible that I cease to describe them! Only pray to God that I may die! away from this fearsome physical and mental pain!"

(Some weeks earlier this pain had been less intense
and had been interpreted as: "Tonight H——t sought
me at 2 and at 5 and I responded!") Not quite two
years later Strindberg died of cancer. I quote from
Heden: "The night of May thirteenth the pains decreased for a while. The dying man patted his daughter
Greta and thanked her with the words, 'Dear Greta!'
Soon the pains started again and the last day was the
most anguished of them all. On Tuesday May fourteenth
at 4.30 P.M. came the end."

Hence the confusions of consciousness, the rationalization of pain, the presentiment of a death that is interpreted as love; the dream and the illusion as defence
for the sleep. Pain leads *not* to consciousness. Pain leads
astray. I make this note because if I had not read the
words Strindberg wrote on "pain" and "seeking" and
thus been able to externalize the story I have written
about pain, then I would not have been able to see
where my words were really leading me. I also wonder
when Strindberg became conscious that it was not
Harriet Bosse but death that was seeking him; if he
became conscious; if he worried about the possible
causal connection. After all—as he always saw his world
ideologically—did he then too assume that God had
heard him pray? Given him a thorn in the flesh? for his
delivery? from life?

In former years we used to tell a funny story about our
friend S. And it was a true story; he himself used to
embroider on it. The joke of the story makes me now—
for reasons that soon will be apparent—less prone to laugh.
I will only give the outlines of the story. The reader is
surely able—if he wants—to put in the comic touches
himself.

We belonged to the same generation both intellectually

and according to our draft cards. The 1940s gave us a disgust for marching boots. When S was drafted and found that there was no honest way of getting out he decided to malinger.

S was a methodical man who studied the technique, the theory and practice of malingering. Before he joined the regiment he had studied all available information on the chief medical officer of the regiment. The man had hoped to become a scientist. Was the only Swede who had made a special study of a rare and disabling form of migraine. It was—in Swedish—called the "helmet of pain." The weeks before S was to appear he therefore sat in the reading room of the Royal Library reading all available literature on this unusual form of headache.

The joke—that which constituted the comic kernel of this funny story—was of course the circumstantial tale of how the doctor step by step was led to discover a "helmet of pain" in this young soldier. His pride. His joy. The laughter exploding in the audience as the true story ended with S being sent home.

On our way home from Peking in 1963, somewhat more than a decade after S had been exempted from military service because of his severe headache, we changed planes in Moscow. Boarded an SAS plane and got Swedish papers. On the front page a photo of S. He is dead of a brain tumour. Gun puts two fingers on the obituary and says:

—Linnaeus!

And I know what she means and as I think about S while we are flying towards Stockholm (and the hostess serves us chicken, salad, red wine and cheese) I see before me printed on yellow paper: "S in Stockholm swears himself free. Evades military service alleging headache. Dies ten years later of tumour in the brain. Great pains. Loud screaming."

S might have been one of the as yet unpublished parts of Linnaeus' *Nemesis Divina.*

This morning I read what I had written. It is quite harmless. Not only for the reader; also for myself. I could keep on in this fashion. Spin out dreams and soul. It would cost me nothing but the manual labour involved. (I dreamt tonight too—I usually dream.) I would never have to face the more unpleasant realities.

About pain: like most people I flee into the experience of physical pain to avoid intellectual conflicts and intellectual discomfort.

A committed suicide in my kitchen a year ago. In the death struggle she had vomited blood over the linoleum floor; the landlord later wrote me and complained. He mourned his linoleum. She was nineteen.

My flat was at Skånegatan 20, Stockholm South. It was on the ground floor. The house was built the first years of this century. When the house was being built my grandfather worked some blocks away. I have inherited a photo where the men can be seen standing in front of the house they had built. They are dressed up. The master builder stands in front of them with a case of beer. My grandfather can be seen to the left. In the right-hand corner you can see the site that would be the house where I got a flat and where A vomited blood over the linoleum.

One room, kitchen, bathroom, running cold water, a stove. Two windows facing north. The windows were glazed with sooty, ever-dirty glass. The first years I had tried to keep them clean; but I gave it up. You never could keep them clean there at the street level. The street was grey and without sunshine. Right across the street a grey rock wall. On top of that, slum buildings that were supposed to have been torn down in the 1920s but had been left standing due to the housing shortage. A tramway passed through the street. Line "Number One." The brick walls around my flat were four feet thick. Never a sound from the neighbours. Dark and quiet.

There A lived before she took her life in the spring of 1963.

Jan, you lie.

On our way home from Peking we had arrived by the Moscow flight to Arlanda-Stockholm. That was January 19, 1963. In the evening some friends telephoned. They wanted us to come over and take a drink. Gun was tired, I went alone. Stockholm was cold winter night all around me as I walked along the quay of the Old Town, and I felt curious about Sweden.

That was the night I met A. She had no place to live. Later on this meeting led to my offering her my flat.

Always remember what it was like being twenty and a drifter. But one forgets. And in remembering you make it romantic. And even if you really are able to develop the picture again and look at it, then it does not matter that you said, at that time:

—Never forget this. Never forget and never forgive. But what help has A of Jan remembering?

It was winter. Because it was always winter when you were young. And I was twenty-two and had come up to Stockholm to collect rejection slips in the publishing houses and to make the rounds of the magazines and try to get rid of some poems. I had not succeeded. The first night in Stockholm I had landed at a party in the northern section of Stockholm. Siberia it was called, by the way. I was hungry but had come late and there was only gin left. I drank half a bottle and spewed out through a window. Then I had to leave the place. I don't remember where I slept.

The next day I had been able to borrow ten crowns from a friend who worked at the Alfort & Cronholm Paint Company. We had shared a tent for a summer some years earlier out at Flaten, south of Stockholm (when I was still younger and had written still more unpublishable poetry. We had taken daywork now and then with bicycle-express companies—it was war and a gasoline shortage—when we needed money. I was sixteen and had quit school in order to become a human being). Now he is master chimney sweep somewhere in Närke province.

I had bacon and beans at a beerhouse, bought cigarettes and washed in the Central Station. Stood in front of a mirror and tried to make myself look respectable. That night I succeeded in staying with a friend who went to the Academy of Fine Arts. He and his girlfriend shared a room. They gave me coffee. We ate. He had some money because he used to make silkscreen posters for grocery stores. I borrowed a mattress. The girl said that I might as well leave. Theirs was only a small room, she said. I agreed, but had nowhere to go so I stayed on and then she shrugged her shoulders and I went to sleep on the mattress.

The next day I walked around in the city and was freezing. Was hungry. Sat in the waiting room of a publishing house for some hours. Then the secretary told me I could go in. The publisher wanted to give me an American novel to translate. But I was proud. Said no. I was a better writer than the American he wanted me to translate, I told the publisher. He said that he just wanted to help me. Be kind. But I was proud. Told him I had no need of help. Then I left. It was afternoon then and greyish dusk and I wondered what would happen. But nothing happened except that it began to snow and the streets were slushy and I stood for some time in the crowd waiting for the tram at Stureplan. The offices had closed and people were going home. I looked into their faces. One of them dropped his paper. I stepped on it and when he had boarded the tram I took it and read it.

Later on I was walking around Ostermalm, where the upper-class people and the embassies could be found. I looked in through the windows. I wondered how they were living. "I watch the animals in their cages," I thought. But I was cold and walked on.

When I noticed that I had come to Norrtull where the road north leaves Stockholm I walked onwards to the northern provinces. Everything was meaningless anyway and in Ådalen, four hundred miles northward, I had a buddy with whom I could stay for some time. It was now very cold and as it was night it was difficult to get a ride. I didn't get a ride until past midnight. It was a girl who was going to Sigtuna. We spoke about France. She too had been hitchhiking there. Then I fell asleep. She woke me up at Märsta. There she let me off.

—We will meet someday, she said.

I was stiff with sleep and my raincoat fluttered in the wind. Her rear lights disappeared and I was alone on the road. No stars and no cars and I walked northward.

The pines along the road were dimly visible as huge masses in the dark. They moved, they marched to and fro across the road. Large columns slowly moving. I understood that I had begun to hallucinate. I do that when I am very tired and hungry and it is dark. I thought I heard a woman scream for help. A light far away. A house. Then I made rural drama with passions and murder in a house that was not there and I became surprised that the human imagination is so stereotyped: "When I at last am so worn down that it can take control, then it has nothing else to give me but a common vulgar novel." At the same time this drama fascinated me. The people, the events, the fright.

Some cars passed, but when I found that they passed right through me I understood that they were ghost cars. Hallucination cars, and I did not care about them. To be on the safe side I began to walk far out on the side of the road anyway, dangerously close to the ditch. It was difficult to distinguish between real cars and hunger cars, I knew that by experience, and I had no wish to be run over. (The last time I shied away from these grey cars with darkened lights that swished by on silent wheels was far up in the Jura in the autumn of 1956. Then I did my last cross-continental hitchhike. I sat at dawn beside the road and told myself:

—Never again.)

Towards morning (I must have slept for a while when walking) I was sitting under the cement stairway of a co-op shop. I took off my boots and tried to make my feet clean with snow. I was as cold as hell and as I had not been able to change socks for a week the skin between my toes had flaked and it bled. A sticky excretion of blood and pus had made the socks stiff like old leather. It hurt when I walked. I wondered what the hell I should do with my life. But the words of that thought came heavily and with long intervals interspersed with dreams.

At dawn that day I was far out on the plains. With the daylight the hallucinations faded out and I only felt the cold and my weariness. I was grateful that the ghost night was over. I got a lift from a milk transport and sat sleeping beside the driver for an hour. That day I continued north. Difficult to get a ride. Much walking. Stayed overnight at a small railroad station on the main line. I was given a cup of coffee and I tried to say something that sounded credible about what I did and why. They did not believe me so my credibility did not amount to much. It didn't matter anyway. They wouldn't have believed me whatever I said. They were nice people though.

They locked me into the waiting room when they went to sleep.

—It is against the regulations.

In the corner there was an iron stove. Coal was used for heating. In the evening it was red-hot with fire and I could see it glow as I fell asleep. The air was dry and musky. In the morning the stove was grey and cold. Then there was hoarfrost on my coat. I had slept soundly and without dreams on the brown wooden bench. When I woke up my eyes smarted. It was difficult to walk. Like walking on knives. Every step hurt. But after I had forced myself to walk for a mile I didn't feel any pain any longer. My cigarettes were finished. I only had a butt.

When I arrived at my buddy's place it was evening and he had some friends there. His wife gave me a pair of socks and I went to their bathroom and washed. I also washed my socks and hung them up to dry. Put on the clean socks and went out to meet their friends. I was in my best form. Told stories, people laughed. We were discussing all night, drinking aquavit with lemonade. I was funny. At the same time I was eating; eating the night through. My friend's wife just carried food to me all the time while I was talking and drinking.

When, looking through a suitcase full of old papers, I find the manuscripts I wrote there that winter, I burn

them. I also find a photo from that winter. My buddy
took it. I stand at the river and am very lean and very
young and have a trench coat and laugh.

In 1963 my flat at Skånegatan in Stockholm was lined
with books. During the last period I had lived there I
had put up bookshelves on every wall in the room,
even under the window; bookshelves all over the entrance hall; bookshelves in the kitchen. I could thus
use the kitchen stove only to boil tea water. As A was
to live there we now packed the books and tore down
the shelves. We were five. The walls rumbled as the
shelves fell.

I had been to the bathroom, I had repaired, painted
and put new tiles on the floor there the summer of
1954. There I had taken down the "Histomap of History:
The Rise and Fall of Peoples and Nations for 4000 Years"
that had been hanging on the wall in the bathroom.
The theory behind this placing of the "Histomap" had
been that every waking minute should be filled with
reason. Unfortunately it proved—what I ought to have
foreseen—that the normal sitting position on the seat
placed the second century before our era at the level
of my eyes. When sitting there I stared into Hellenism.
When pissing, standing, then I looked at Hyksos kings,
Hittites and the Hsia dynasty. Only if I went on my
knees, with my head over the bowl, being drunk and
sick, could I see more contemporary events. But I am
seldom that drunk. This could seem like a thought.
But was not. Just chance.

As I came out from the bathroom A stood against
the wall of the hall. I told this to her as a funny
story—though I don't see the deeper meaning in it any
longer—and she didn't listen. She was staring into the
room where they were toppling the bookshelves from

the left-hand wall. Ninety feet of history, of literature, fell to the floor. We all laughed. But not A. I can see her standing at the wall with her palms pressed against the pattern of the wallpaper behind her.

I have just been listening to the Handel Chamber Trio in G Major. It usually helps. I bought the record in Hong Kong and took it along to Peking. It belongs to my mental first-aid kit. But now in the silence when there is but a low humming noise in the loudspeakers and I hear a fox howl far away in the forest I feel the irritation still clawing the sinews of my neck and the disgust is like a sour film on my teeth. I turn the record and let his C Minor Sonata for Oboe and Cembalo rinse the room.

The big loudspeakers are standing there under the windows at the back wall. The bookshelves muffle all echoes and the work lamp throws a sharp cone of yellow light over the typewriter and my hands. Just as I close my eyes the dance comes. At last the irritation gives way. I lean back in the chair and I am all alone with Handel and the eighteenth century.

I need music. Without liquor and music this life would be unbearable. But I consume more music than alcohol. Partly because music is cheaper and partly because music is better for my health; I don't wake up with a hangover after a night's heavy listening. As I write this I betray to myself that I am neither clear nor consistent in my attitude towards art. I usually speak about the formation of consciousness through art; the intellectual function. But I treat Handel as if he were Librium, a tranquillizing pill. Of course I am able to express it more beautifully; music liberates.

Since my adolescence music has been a need. And the only funny thing about it was that all grownups and all

teachers during my whole childhood stubbornly main-
tained that I was absolutely lacking in any musical
sense. Later on I understood that this probably was due
to our experiencing music in diametrically different
ways. I am not saying that my way is better. Just that
it is.

These were typewriter thoughts. I once again felt the
irritation I tried to get rid of. Then—when I closed my
eyes and felt the tensions relax a whole chain of thought-
fragments whirled away in the music. The music had
dissolved the anger and let my thoughts loose. The
dialection of art. The revolt and creativeness of Handel.
The Beggar's Opera as revolt against Handel. The link
to Hogarth and Goya in this revolt. The *Dreigrosch-
enoper* of Brecht as the loving rejection of the rejected.
The tremendous historical irony that Brecht's anti-hit
later on becomes a true hit and slops out of all the
jukeboxes in the (Western) world after Brecht's own
death. He utilized the form of the hit to reveal the real
function of "popular music," that of hiding reality, and
this then becomes a new hit that a new generation will
sing to forget its reality: "Mack the Knife."

I have committed sociability today. And I can't stand
that any longer. One sits. And one smiles with one's
lips. And one grins forth in efforts to say nice things—
things, not thoughts. It wouldn't do to hurt or disturb.
Sometimes I find that I have just shut them off completely. I don't even know what they are talking about
in the room, fifteen minutes have passed while I was
turned off. But I seem to be able to manage the ordinary cultured grunting noises even without consciousness. Rather—consciously I would not have been
able to manage them for any length of time. I hate those
days when I have to meet people like this, be sociable,
without any contact, without getting anything rational

said or done. To sit at a table in communal mastication and buzz your voice.

Gun says that I have to keep myself on edge, have to pretend. Afterwards she praises me. Our guests had not noticed how I despised them. Gun is good, she is the most rational of the women I have met. But even she has this need to meet people. She needs people to talk to. She reads women's magazines too. But I have managed to get rid of most of those I consider burdensome. Don't misunderstand now. I like my friends. Those with whom I can be myself. Eat meat, drink aquavit, sing; I like all that. I also like the sharp discussions. Sometimes I have sat for up to twenty hours in one continuous discussion. Then this good tension of feeling how you are changing, fertilized, remoulded. I meet, I want to meet, people for three reasons: work, intellectual contact and old friendship. The rest is evil.

I am not impolite. I worked at an office for two years once. I succeeded even there in keeping at a distance. I did my job. Did it well too. Spoke, was friendly; I even joked with the others who worked in the same room but I managed so completely to avoid being involved in their lives that I forgot their names the very day I left.

But the parasitical sociability is the most common in our culture. That which is not honest, not intellectual. Which just wastes time. Today this made me so irritated that I became childish and, like thirty years ago, thought over and over again: "If only they would disappear, dissolve, sink through the floor, blow away. Just leave me in peace."

Life is short. Company steals time. And this, my time, is all I have. I try to get Gun to understand. I say:

—Why do you want to see them? We don't need to hurt them, we can just make ourselves invisible, inaccessible. Smile in a friendly manner if we see them and then just slide away. You know how they are. I could write every damned line they speak before they arrive. I could have given you a detailed script of this whole destroyed afternoon. They can't give us anything.

Gun says that they are friendly. She relaxes with them. To me they are only disturbing, destructive. I am unable to work for a whole day after such an afternoon. I feel sick.

—I just want to be left in peace, I say to Gun. Can you never understand? Only to be in peace and work.

She does not make any answer. She just goes up the stairs. I let the music spin this cocoon of peace and solitude around me.

I am not able to accept this description of my relations to my environment. It is romantic, hence a lie. As my reactions to human contact came to play a role for A it is necessary to undress JM.

Of course, the fact is that I don't dare to meet people. They come too close to me.

Every meeting is a possibility for passion and tragedy. The passion is a tragedy. I have always been clumsy. I have never been able to learn the rules of the social game. I felt them as strange rules even as a child. If I don't hide behind my glasses I might forget myself, come close to people, be dragged into their lives.

I know very well what I experienced the fifteen minutes I was absent. I sat in my comfortable green chair, the cup of coffee was standing on the yellow table beside me. The girl was sitting on the blue couch in front of me. We had two guests. Man and wife. As I was talking I looked up and saw the girl. She sat there in clear outline in front of me. She had a red skirt and it had slipped up over her knees as she sat down. I got all dry in my mouth. While I was talking (cultured grunt-ing noise) she looked at me. She had brown eyes.

No, I was not in love. But at that moment I wanted her. I wanted her badly. There was nothing special about her, she was friendly and rather pretty and not directly stupid. She was not a woman I could stand. If I woke up one morning and found her beside me in bed I would have no idea of what to talk to her about. It was just a sudden flash of contact. I suppose that everybody feels the same. (At other times it might be a sudden flash of anger or hate or sorrow.)

As a child it seemed to me as if others were able to handle such situations in a different way. When I was young I used to say that they had society in their blood. For myself I have always had to keep the rules of the game in my head. You can call it the conscious life if you wish. The one where you have your eternal freedom. But then this consciousness is rather painful.

I know what can happen. I have been through it too many times. But where others manage their lives with conditioning, reflexes and inhibitions, I always found myself forced to make conscious decisions.

This has made me nearsighted. Because as a child there was only one way for me to avoid facing these decisions: to throw reality out of focus. Every time I was in a difficult situation I blurred reality around me. I was also eidetic; at nights I could redevelop reality and it would then be a more distinct and more colourful reality than any real reality ever could be. I can still do that. But now I have to strain myself to be able to do it; or else be very tired. Therefore it was wrong of me to write that I "hallucinated" cars. I have always known the border between the reality of visions and dreams and the reality of reality.

But I find it difficult to keep the rules of the game in mind and follow them. And I know the consequences of not following them. So I prefer being alone or in relaxing company where you drink aquavit and are happy.

The need for loneliness is not only due to this easily explainable reluctance for close contacts. I have also, ever since I was very young—as far back as I can remember—felt the urge to be alone. This is misunderstood. In English the very word "loneliness" bears a negative charge. The idea that the state of being all one (alone—Swedish, *alena*) is positive has to be expressed with the Latinized "solitude." Very early—I can't have been more than four or five years old—I realized that I must make up excuses to be left alone. If I said straight out that I wanted to be left alone ("leave me in peace") the surrounding people all came forward and said they wanted to understand me; something must be the matter; and they patted me on the head and they bowed down and had their big grinning faces in front of me and smiled (so I could see their yellow teeth) and said:

—Jan, little Jan, whatever is the matter?

As a child you have to lie to be left alone. But I just wanted to be alone. The only relative I had who understood this was my maternal uncle Folke. He never cared the least for me and he rarely spoke to me. Thus I came to like him.

You also need to be alone when you change; when you know that you are going to change you seek loneliness. As I feel intellectual work to be a continuous change of personality I feel the need for periods of deep loneliness.

Gun disturbs me too. At nights I sit and look at slides of Timurid tilework. The projector sings beside me, the hot air sweeps by me and there on the wall dead masters draw mighty geometrical patterns of tile-work. Overpoweringly beautiful and pure. I hold the fragments of tiles in my hands, touch the cracked glazing with my fingertips and the Timuridian renaissance is an ache in my body. Then Gun sleeps and the dog lies on the bearskin fell at my feet. And I am quite alone and the art, colour and form, is a pain of beauty. There is also a third reason that is very rational. I write. The more friends I have the more motifs become tabu. In order to write freely I must be free from the corrupting influence of friendships.

All this might be true. And as far as the actual situation is concerned it is true. Still, it is only a defensive truth. I have a guilty feeling about A. And I can't forget that she phoned me and wanted to talk to me. She wanted to invite me out to a restaurant. To talk, she said, she needed to talk. But I had no time. I was writing about the Timurids. Had no time. Did not want to either.

The linoleum on the kitchen floor at Skånegatan had a geometrical pattern. Imitation tilework, arabesque. As a pattern it didn't interest me. I found it dull. When I lived there I kept the floor covered with a real Afghan kelim. A rustically honest geometrical pattern. I took that rug away when A moved in.

A destroyed the naked linoleum. In her death struggle she flushed it with her blood and even if that pattern had been sham and imitation I now feel difficulties in reviving the overpowering purity of the Timurid tile-work. The original.

I try to tell myself that all this does not concern me. The Timurid tilework is soiled with blood too. Not by the blood of a single girl but by the blood of the count-less dead. "A European from the twentieth century can hardly understand how men could be found to fulfil such of Timur's orders as that of building a tower consisting of two thousand living human beings placed one upon another and smothered by clay and fragments of tile." So wrote the innocent Barthold in 1912.

But that does not help me. As I now project the beautiful tilework of the Timurids on the wall A lies convulsed across that pure form, her nails scratch the joints and there is blood foaming from her mouth. It doesn't help me that I can find beautifully written histories from the wars of Timur.

Strike out and go on.

A is standing there at the wall of the hall. The palms of her hands and the back of her head against the pattern of the wallpaper. We have torn down the shelves. The books have been carried away in the Skipper's car. We laugh. There is a cloud of dust in the room. We are sweaty and drink beer.

—You haven't cleaned this place for many years, you damn bastard, says the Skipper.

Now when I see A standing at the wall I clearly remember that day in August 1954. Then too I stood in this door. Where A is now standing hung a grey coat.

Late in fall 1953 I had arrived in Sweden. In the spring of 1954 I moved into this flat. I worked at an office from eight in the morning to four in the afternoon. I took no lunch. At night I wrote.

In January 1954 I had published my first drama. Privately printed. It was weak. In the spring of 1954 I got my first novel accepted. It was to be published in

September 1954. That summer I was alone in my flat. I was waiting for the woman I then loved. I paint the walls. I put in a new floor in the bathroom. Lay the tiles myself. I try to make the whole small flat look nice. I have bought furniture on credit and with intense concentration I try to fashion what is called "a home." The girl I then loved wanted such a thing, I understood. I looked at the way people had furnished their dwellings, saw her reactions when we visited them, and now I was hard at work to create a facsimile in this flat. I wanted her to be comfortable.

The books then covered the long wall in the room. That made her afraid. I put them in double rows to make three walls free for her home. She could hang paintings there. I did as well as I could, I thought.

A moment ago the sun shone and summer glittered on the water and the small town mirrored the red castle idyllically in the lake. Now overcast, haze, soon will come the rain. Already the water has become dull and leaden.

To observe these changes; to run in the forests with my dog; to lean down and study the anthills; all this can be described—is often described—as the unchangeable spring. But the unchangeability of it hides lies and illusions. In the summer of 1954 I used to rent a boat at the Eriksdal bath and row to the Årsta Isles. There I lay on the meadow sleeping with the birches over me and the city—far away—surrounding me. When I opened my eyes I could see the sun shining through the leaves. It is quite difficult for me now to see birch leaves as I saw them then.

I read Seume that summer. Johann Gottfried. On the inside cover I had printed in small letters: "The Candidian fate. As true autobiography. The rational man becomes in the Germany of petty princelings: '*Gries-grämig, misswollend, negativ.*' Where not?" I couldn't stand Goethe at that time. I had read him and always disliked him. The classic of German misery. The soul of a pug dog. The only thing I had in common with him was the interest in model railroads. Goethe played with model trains in his old age, I in my childhood.

What Goethe said about Seume: sour, evil-minded, negative, rude; that I considered the highest praise a writer could get. Goethe made an Italian tour, but Seume walked to Syracuse.

Since then I have changed. I still feel more akin to Seume: "*Griesgrämig, misswollend, negativ, sansculot-tisch.*" But in China I learned to read Goethe. Still with great reserve. He was a bootlicker. That was not neces-sary. There were other German writers who knew their worth. But he wrote a couple of readable things.

What still strikes me as funny though is to see all these revolutionary Germans who fall flat on their stomachs in front of the *Geheimrat.* The revolutionary German— or Swede—is usually a state councillor that has gone astray.

In that summer of 1954 when I was expecting my then beloved I had rowed out to the Årsta Isles, lain in the grass and read Seume. And the words were wholesome in this idyllic summer: "Fate has kicked me around. I am not so stubborn that I seek to enforce my views against the millions; but I am independent enough not to deny them when faced with the millions and their first and their last."

If all this was true, that is another and far sadder story. But such was my ideal self.

What are you actually describing? A has already committed suicide many pages ago. She vomited blood

on your kitchen floor and you sailed away into the
Timuridian renaissance. She had borrowed your flat. You
had not had an affair with her. What about it?

It is this. She stands in the hallway and I look at her.
That had quite a lot to do with her death. I knew then
when I saw her that she would die. Let me return to
1954:

Just where A was standing hung a grey coat. Above
the coat was a hatrack. To the far right hung my raincoat. On the hatrack lay a newspaper. The grey coat was
hairy. Like an animal. It was modern at that time. I take
the step out into the hall, hear my then woman (she had
now arrived and moved into this facsimile of a home—
long story that I strike out) in the room. She is breathing. She is reading. I see her coat, the grey, hairy one,
hanging in front of me in the hall. I go up to it and take
the letter out of her coat pocket. The envelope is blue.

I knew that it would be there. It had haunted her
during the quarrel. The moment I felt the envelope between my fingers I suspected that she had let it peep
forth with a blue envelope corner out of the coat pocket
in order to ensure that I would take it. I find the situation uncomfortable. I take the letter and read it.

As soon as I see the letter thrust its corner up out of
the pocket I know what I am going to do; I know what
there is to read in the letter; I know how I will react.
This knowledge gives me no freedom. The knowledge,
I think, is like the knowledge a railroad car has about
the tracks it runs on.

I read the letter. I find it strange that such a letter—
I myself have also written them—has such a totally
different effect when you yourself are neither sender
nor receiver but only the third party. It would be sane
and reasonable to put it back again in its envelope and
stick the envelope back in the pocket. Reasonable and

calm. It would also frighten her in there. But I don't
do so. I know that I won't do it. Anyway, everything is
unavoidable. Now and always. The rolling railroad car
might be conscious of the tracks and hear the throbbing
as it crashes over the joints, but the live force is too
large and it rolls on. I will stage a scene of jealousy. The
consciousness of this disgusts me.

As long as possible, I stay in the hall. I listen to her
breathing. It has changed rhythm. Now she only pre-
tends to read, she is marking reading with her breathing
but she turns no pages. She is listening to me.

I stand for another couple of seconds in the hall before I enter the room. Beforehand I experience all that
is going to happen. Once more I think: If I were really
rational I would shut off all emotions, take a deep breath
and walk into the room and take a cup of coffee with
her. But it is impossible. I am in a state of emotional
tension. I observe my pulse, it is quickening, my mouth
has become dry, a harsh feeling against my tongue; the
light drumming noise in my ears. I am *cocu*. Swindled, betrayed. But that is nothing special. I have been so before, I will be again.

But I am responsible. She has messed it up. She sits
in there in that room like a fly caught in a spider web.
I wonder if she in reality had wanted me to read that
letter in order to get me to act, tearing the web.

My body is reacting. I am aware that I will not at all
be able to keep the talk on a rational and humanly
reasonable level. (As if there existed such a level.) But
I don't want to hurt her.

I walk into the room and she looks at me. (There a
contact with A. The same big eyes, the same roe-deer
stare.) Actually I am very agitated. All muscles in high
tonus, dry throat, an ill-boding springiness of gait.
And what am I to do? I can't in good conscience beat

my breast and be the injured one. That much of a hypocrite I am not. I myself was unfaithful to her not long
ago. And even if I—being careful in my promises—have
not put anything on paper, the words I have uttered are
witnesses against me. I hear them sounding in my ears.

But neither can I control my emotions. Everything is
inevitable. Just as I pass the threshold I try to hold on
to an intellectual judgment of the situation. In rapid
succession thoughts come: "Brother, you always speak
about rationality. Here is Rhodos, jump here . . . *hic
salta* . . . *salto mortale,* leap of death. The grandeur of
the leap of death is that it succeeds. The double *salto
mortale* is the journeyman test for the balanced and well-
trained acrobat. So jump!"

But I pass the threshold and enter the room and am
incapable of any leap. Then we look at each other. She
says:

—What is the matter?

At the same time her eyes become very black as her
pupils open large.

—I don't mind being swindled, I say. (That is a lie,
of course. I have very much against being swindled,
but it is a wording that is to bring out the rest of the
thought in sharper contrast.) But God damn me, I dislike being exploited. This office work, this home was a
self-imposed bondage. A yoke I bore. But I am not
giving up my freedom to support your lovers.

I am aware that I stand on the floor and talk. That is
the last refuge. When there is no longer any possibility
of keeping a rational control and I feel how the situation
glides out of my hands and my fingers lose their grip
and straighten out, then I talk as a last defence.

(I won't say anything about the letter. I won't write
about our conflict. I didn't have and I do not have any
right to moralize. Believe me.)

—Don't beat me, she says.

She is now standing. Moving backwards. Coming close to the wall. Pushing her palms against the wallpaper. Her lips are white and she says:

—Don't beat me to death, don't beat me to death.

—No, I never hit you.

Because I never do hit. I never have beaten her. I usually don't beat people. Partly because I am strong enough (fear) to be able to kill with my hands. But she only looks into my eyes and says over and over again in a monotonous voice:

—Please, don't kill me. Please, don't kill me. Please, don't kill me.

While we have been saying this I have been standing quite still just inside the threshold. Outside the window a tram can be heard. I then see our future as clearly as if I had written it. But that doesn't help. I take the little plaster of Paris torso that is standing in the bookshelf. It is ugly. I have always found it ugly. It is hers. It has been given to her. As I hold it in my right hand I understand that I am going to smash it. A woman's torso. The work of a student from the sculptor section of the Academy of Fine Arts. (Who never amounted to anything and never quite became an artist, by the way.)

While I am watching my right hand stretch out and see my fingers taking hold around the torso and the arm bending as the torso lifts, I think: He who is without sin, let him cast the first stone. And as I am not I throw it.

I turn the figure around in my hand and then I hurl it towards the records. They are standing there in their cases in their hundreds and I smash fifty of them in that throw. I love them. They are blues on original labels. (A month later I will play some of the remaining ones

for another woman and then I will carry her to the bed
and she will say:

—Jan, Jan, I love you.

I probably knew that already then. But I didn't know
who it would be. I do not plan. I only know what is to
happen. So is it written. I have the key to the exercises.)
She has sat down on the bed now in 1954 and
whimpers. I am suddenly very tired. As the records fall
in broken pieces, clattering, to the floor there is only
tiredness in my body.

—You did that in order not to strike me, she says.

—Yes, I say. It must have been so.

I sit down in the chair, the green one.

—You must understand me, she says.

—But I do, I say. Though it hurts.

Then she begins talking of her bad conscience. I
dislike that. Nothing can be solved with morals and
conscience. That is a wide road. Nothing is cheaper
than remorse. The inevitable is the tragic. To stop her
and to get rid of her self-reproaches I say:

—It is nothing strange. You don't believe I have
been faithful, do you? When I was away working for
three days I spent them with E.

Now she stops reproaching herself. She starts to
cry loudly instead. Comes up to me and tries to claw
my face with her nails. I keep hold of her hands, she
spits in my face, kicks, hisses, weeps, says:

—Must you always say everything? Must you understand everything? Must you know everything?

I am very tired. It all seems so meaningless to me.
Everything is being enacted just as I had written it—
line by line—as soon as I first saw the blue envelope
jutting out of the pocket of that hairy grey coat.

—Life hurts, I say.

But as I hold her and feel her pulse under my fingers the mood changes. And without any real tran-
sition from hatred to love we are in the middle of
coitus. Her head is thrown back, her eyes are closed
and her mouth half open. Our quarrels usually ended
that way. Even if only very few of our coital scenes
started with quarrels. But the act gets a cold, porno-
graphic outline. And anyway I know that all is over.
Later on I carry her to the bed and she lies softly
crying. I stroke her hair and feel great tenderness
towards her and know that I am finished with her.

When I see A standing there at the wall with her
palms on the wallpaper I remember the large and
blackening eyes of 1954 and feel disheartened.

My untruthfulness is like alum over my skin. I depict my quite normal and rather trite and petty behaviour as heroics. And this without doing it in such a
manner that I am able to catch myself in barefaced
lying. The words and the sequence of events were
true. But I distrust and dislike the colouring.

What was really unpleasant with this blue envelope
was the consciousness that I experienced outside myself. And the inevitability with which I reacted despite
knowing the whole time both how I was going to
react and the consequences of my reactions.

The inevitability of A and her eyes. Her palms. The
inevitability.

Soon before A took her life I was in the flat to collect my belongings, the last I had there. It surprised
me that I could not smell her odor in the room. She
was not at home. I had let myself in with my own
key. It was a frozen and girlish room. The bed stood
in the middle of the floor. Large photos of herself on

the walls. Small tablecloths of lace, small ornaments. Outside, the grey street and the rumbling tram. She had a shelf full of poetry. She read poetry. I stood for a while and looked at the photo she had taken of herself. It underlined longing and eyes. This worried me. Again I remembered her standing in the hall. When I was to leave I took up my keys and put them on her bedside table. They lay in the centre of the lacework. Then I left and slammed the door shut behind me.

In this account A appears only as a catalyst. Her suicide brought about a rapid dissolution of my consciousness. The duplicity of that consciousness was brought into the open; thereby it started to dissolve. The process was surely unavoidable in any case, but when A took her life, it intervened directly in my sphere of action and forced me to ask questions I had to answer.

This does not mean that I downgrade A as a human being. But I am not writing her life. I do not give the background to her actions. Not because that background is unknown to me or because I am unable to comprehend her situation or because that situation is without interest for me; but because that work for me in my situation just now would be an act of fleeing (a flight of fancy).

The book on A: "A Swedish tragedy." The young girl, beautiful, intelligent; reading poetry.

—It is strange, she once said, I never find a good man. I only attract men I don't care for. Men who only say I am beautiful. The men I like never care for me.

I have seen the cartoon many times. The beautiful girl who says, "But you don't care for my soul." And in our culture we are all supposed to find that very funny. She was too good-looking to be able to find the men she wanted.

The social necessity with which she was hunted to death. The homelessness, the immobility of a bureaucratic society doomed her. She was a weak animal in an indifferent culture and the dogs of reality were snapping at her heels as she was fleeing. She died of a well-ordered society. But that is another novel.

A rang me up. That was some days before she committed suicide. It was a morning in early spring. I sat at my typewriter. The telephone stood on my left. The water in the bay was deep blue, the air was clear that day, a cold scent as of autumn over the fields.

—Do I disturb you? she asked.

—No, of course you don't, I said.

But I was lying. Of course she interrupted my work. But I answered politely:

—No, you don't disturb.

She wanted to take me and Gun out to a restaurant. Take us out for an evening. She wanted to pay. Talk. I did not want to.

—Not now, I said. Some other time. Later.

Partly I held that she had too little money, her salary was too low to take me out. I didn't want to exploit her gratitude. Partly because I don't let myself be invited out. I can't remember when I let someone pay for me in a restaurant last. I am not an expense-account eater. And I don't want to become corrupted by gratitude.

But the main reason was that I was then cutting off unnecessary personal contacts. I attended a meeting— the adult education association—some time ago. They spoke about the need for "areas of contact." I feel no such need. Consciousness is a need, integrity is a need. But "contact" in general has no value to me whatsoever.

Let me explain. I am a writer. I am an intellectual. My task is to make others conscious, to express and word, thus influence and change others. That is my role. I might often doubt that what I do is of value; but if it can at all have some value, then the work achieves its value only as long as I—the tool of my work—am not lured away.

In order not to hurt people I have to tamper with my insight. Already as a child you are told that there are truths you had better keep for yourself. But it is inconvenient to falsify yourself to suit others. And there is a great danger in lying to yourself. You become an addict. Illusions are like narcotics. In utilizing the commonplace lies of our culture you will soon find that you can't live without them. The life lie. The breaking of this habit is painful.

When I sit in a restaurant with people I feel the situation to be that of a complicated game of chess. My words have to be chosen, facial expressions adjusted, I must utilize this contact for a reasonable purpose. It should be useful, rational and useful for the rational. Chess is a bad likening; to play, to win—all that is meaningless. But I find nothing better just now. It at least gives the feeling of strained attention.

I haven't always felt like this. Contact and human relations are popular in our culture. Books are filled with the phrases. And when I was sufficiently young I believed in the written words. I assumed that good human relations were fruitful. But I found that if I was to bear any fruit after these contacts then I would bear suburban gardens, model railroads, football, prejudices about race, the low life. That sort of human relationship is one-sided. I cannot give insight. I only become blunted. When playing the game you have to follow the rules. And if the rules are wrong you are beaten from the beginning. And your victory will then be your own defeat. Only the carefully selected contact is fruitful.

(I have reason to consider nearly everything that my contemporaries imagine to be true, accepted, real as only hallucinations, lies and self-deception.)

As you understand, I am now defending myself. I did *not* want to talk to A. And that unwillingness was not a fear of falling in love—as I tried to convince myself some pages back—it was a more general fear of contact.

I was very lonely. And thus I have, since I returned to Sweden in January 1963, in a planned manner broken with my friends. I do not want to be fettered. At the same time I have also tried to free myself from the fetters of hatred. I have had reason to dislike (or hate, which is a better word) different people. At the same time as I have broken with my friends I have thus established neutral relationships to my enemies. So I liberate myself from all contacts.

B wrote an extremely vicious novel about me. We had known each other from 1950 to around 1954. Had been hitchhiking through France, lived in the eastern Pyrenees, known each other quite well. In 1960 B published the novel. It came at a bad time. It did hurt me. Financially it broke several possibilities for me. At that time I had no paper in which to write and there was a running press campaign against me. One man was fired from the Swedish Radio because he had let me speak about the third world. It was the best novel that B had —up to now—written. But it was a vicious book filled with personal hatred. At the same time as it painted a picture of an individual that everybody recognized as being a picture of JM (and the critics wrote about it

as being a picture of JM) it was in every detail false.
When I read it I was struck by it. I had never believed
that B was able to feel such strong emotion as the
hatred in that book. It was a good book. B telephoned
me, said:

—They say I have written a book about you. Have
you read it?

I said:

—It is the best you have written.

I never did hit back. I have not written about B.
The book had hurt me and my work but it was a good
book. In a couple of years the personal would pass and
the book would remain.

Now I invite B to lunch. We drink good red wine.
We talk. Nothing is mentioned. I am free of all fetters.

Strange. You freeze without fetters. No friends and no
enemies. This hurts. As I write this the house is quite
empty. A shell around me. Outside the windows the leaf-
bud-green haze of the birches shimmers in the wind and
the white stems stand marching towards the blue bay.
Only my typewriter coughs in the quietness. It is very
empty. And those who mean something for me are now all
dead. They stand closely packed in their shelves.

Certainly it happens that I wish I were nineteen again
and we all were friends and talked. But our lives have
changed. And already at that time we were drifting away
from each other. I found that what we had talked about
and said we meant, the others had not meant but only
talked about. They sat there one day with their wives and
children and lawn mowers and no longer took life seriously. But I knew that they once had known and experienced this seriousness.

How bloody pathetic can you become, Jan?

When I was nineteen I sat talking with L in his room.
He was unhappy. He spoke about his unhappiness. He
wanted to hang himself. After three hours he had convinced me. As he was and as he experienced the world
and as his future would develop, it would be rational to
hang himself. When he told me he would go up to the
attic and hang himself I said goodbye, shook his hand and
left. Man has the freedom of choice.

He went upstairs to the attic and hanged himself. Our
common friends who in theory had always said that they
believed in choice and reason did not understand my behaviour.

—Don't you understand that I have respect for the integrity of my friends? I said.

But they could not feel that way.

L was cut down. Not by me. I had gone before he
hanged himself. He was cut down by chance. His was not
a suicide for show. His mother—who was a teacher—had
got the afternoon off due to an unforeseen accident in
the class, she arrived home two hours earlier than usual,
and as she went to the attic to fetch linen she found L.

So L was cut down. He was taken to the hospital. To
the insane asylum; they gave him insulin shocks and elec-
tric shocks and they did a frontal lobotomy and they put
him through narcoanalysis and psychoanalysis and had
psychologists and social workers attending him. Then he
was let out after some years. They say that he is quite
capable of both dressing and undressing himself now.

But all this he had told me the afternoon he was
planning to hang himself.

—That is the way it will go with me. I don't want it to
happen. I, I, the I sitting here and now, don't want this
to happen to me.

In the first two attempts to write this book there followed here a discussion about the brothers Goncourt. L had quoted them that afternoon. They were among our literary ideals. From the diary L quoted what Edmond had written as Jules was deteriorating, becoming a "thing," dying. That was a true story. L did that. L spoke about many things that afternoon. The Goncourts and his own fear of insanity (which was well founded). About a girl we both knew. About his homosexual experiences—of which I had known nothing. He had been seduced by a man working for the British Council. An affair that seemed to consist of poetry and language and lovemaking and comradeship between men.

In this affair he had lost his assurance of his own sexual role. I tried to tell him that that did not matter very much. He could choose it. The homosexual role is a little bit more difficult in our culture but in Sweden at least it is not criminal. It is thus a difficult but not impossible role.

But he did not want to listen to this argument. What he really meant was that he was beginning to be unable even to distinguish his sexual role. He was depersonalizing. He was disintegrating in all fields.

I did not write that in the former editions. I used the Goncourts as a (true) cover story. Now I understand why. The story I had told about L and the hanging was correct. But I gave it the colouring of my utter conviction of being in the right. As a matter of fact I had no such conviction. In later years, when thinking about L, I have wondered whether his speaking of his homosexual experiences had activated such prejudices in me (unconscious) that I became prone to push him up towards the attic. Honestly, I don't know. That is a

very painful suspicion. But all the same—seeing L
today I think it is a pity that his mother cut him down.
He is a Jules that went on living, though already dead.

The wind is rising. The woodwork creaks. The sunshine
is hard and objective. Cold light. The spring is not romantic. It is autumn, overgrown green and corrupt, which
is romantic. Decay. Smell of death. Spring is coldly rational. Then nothing is hidden. What was covered with
snow then lies bared; the earth bluish black and naked
under the sun.

If lack of contact and loneliness were the same as isolation and turning inwards it would be without use. But it
is observing, looking on, looking out, and thus the capacity
for feeling with others. Lack of emotional entanglement
is the basis for sympathy. This is of course an old psycho-
analytic thought. Freud himself was hardly known for his
gregariousness.

With contact your sight is blurred, you get lost in illusions, lose your capability to look outwards, and behave
foolishly. That is, thoughtlessly and short-wittedly.

So I said:

—Not now. Another time. Phone me again.

And I observed. And I knew. And she never phoned
again. And I knew.

But this time without consciously reflecting on my observation and my acts. It was now 1963, and not 1946
when I had acted consciously with sympathy.

A only disturbed me by calling. Disturbed me in my
work.

All this I have written about isolation flows so smoothly.
It is almost convincing. But it is more rationalization than
rational.

The plain truth is that I am tired and afraid. Very frightened and dead tired. It is painful to have to wake up in the morning and face the day. In an attempt to convince me that I am sleeping I pull the beautifully embroidered sheepskin fell over my head. Feel the white fleece against my eyelids and lie quite still as if I did not exist. Then my bladder and my bowels and the birds singing outside the windows and the telephone ringing beside me force me to become conscious of existing and I am forced out of bed.

The house out here at Fagervik is beautifully situated. A moraine slope from the pine forest down to the lake. Spruces and birches and a wide view over the lakes and meadows. Far in the background the old city with its red castle and white church and beyond that the green wall of forest. In this moraine slope I sit like in a burrow. But if all the entrances are watched even the fox will be caught. One is caught even in the deepest of burrows. You know how it is. You breathe heavily, you have been running far through the scrubby forest. You lie in the furthest retreat far inside the dark, your ears prick up and you listen.

And you say to yourself that you are free and alone and if you don't say that, you say that you are ahead. And that is quite true, you are ahead like the fox is ahead of the hounds.

My fear is of course influenced by my personal traits, my qualities and illusions; still, it is an objective fear valid for all of us. With the weapon systems now in construction and the missiles hiding and the radar warnings and the small stupid minds that direct these weapons, we all are in danger of being slaughtered by mistake.

The mistake is improbable. But the improbability becomes a certainty if the time factor is taken into account. We will all be killed off because of our damn stupidity.

Sheep being led to the slaughter, but not struggling. Even
a rat will fight back when he is cornered. I hope humanity
will rise to the rat-level of consciousness.

You need consciousness and reason to turn this inevitability. I wrote about Freud. He believed in reason: "Still
the situation is not as hopeless as it might seem just now.
No matter how powerful the emotions and vested interests may be, the intellect is also a power, not exactly the
one that wins in the short run, but surely in the long."
But this was written concerning psychoanalysis and was
written before August 1914.

For us the cold remark that Freud made at the New
Year's Eve of 1900 has taken on a different—and more
repugnant—meaning than he intended it to have: "The
new century—I dare say that what interests us most about
it is that it contains the date of our death . . ."

The hall was rather dark. When I stepped out of the
bathroom and came to see A standing there I felt a sudden
fear. The laughter from the room where my friends were
tearing down the bookshelves suddenly ceased. I heard
A breathing and the singing of water in the pipes. In this
moment of dark and isolated quiet I felt that A was not
only very weak, she was also very scared and very hunted.
Then I knew.

Now afterwards it would be easy to say that this knowledge is a postfact construction. But it is not so. The feeling had a strong taste of *déjà vu*. Where A stood she
formed the outline of the grey coat. And in 1963 as in
1954 there was the fear of the inevitability of consciousness.

After 1954 I left Sweden. I had been there from the
late fall of 1953 and tried to work in an office, live as
others live, buy furniture on credit, go to simple restau-
rants and forget that reality existed. But after 1954 I left

Sweden and didn't come back until just before the 1956 autumn of Suez and Hungary. Then I stayed in Stockholm for half a year.

At that time I made fun of the grey coat. I built bookshelves even in the hall and in the kitchen. The books filled the flat from floor to roof. They were creeping forth over the doors, shelves slowly filling the doorways. One had to bow low in order to go from the hall to the room; in the kitchen the stove had become useless. (I didn't build alone, Gun and my friend S built—they were artists and had good hands for building—I sorted the books.) That time I amused myself by letting the outline of the grey coat form a frame around a very special section of my library. That was quite a private joke; I fill my existence with such private jokes—they make the everyday surroundings charged with power—simple and normal objects get transformed and receive associations and that helps in keeping me conscious. Gun, who was sawing and hammering and painting, knew nothing about it. But I was happily (and piercingly) whistling when I put up the books in the hall.

That was the section of false insights. There I had placed most of the theology. There stood the learned works on ESP. There had been gathered the later works of Wilhelm Reich. (That had been a difficult decision. He had impressed me tremendously when I first read him during the war. His earlier works, *The Sexual Revolution* and *The Mass Psychology of Fascism*, I let stay in the section for psychology and of the late works I placed *Listen, Little Man* in the section for German literature.) There stood the full stenographic records of the Moscow trials. Grey bindings. There stood the three red volumes of *The Witches' Hammer, Malleus Maleficarum,* by Jacob Sprenger and Heinrich Institoris (the German language edition, Berlin 1906). The clear logic of the Inquisition.

Well, that these books came to be placed inside the outline of the grey coat was a private joke. Nobody else could—and nobody else was allowed to—see the joke. It was a sick joke all for my own benefit. Because what had made me afraid when I had stepped out of the bathroom and seen the blue envelope jutting out of the pocket of the hairy grey coat (and what later would make me afraid when I would see A standing inside the outline of that coat) was that I had known. The borders between what I had known, what I suddenly knew and what I was going to know were so dim and so floating that I am not even long afterwards able to say, with any degree of surety, what was an objective development—a flow of developments outside myself and outside my possibilities of interference—and what was a development directed by me. An acting to which I had written the lines and coached the performers. Therefore: insight (true or false) gives guilt.

Just where the blue envelope had been jutting out I put the three red volumes of *The Witches' Hammer*:

"One is to take care, and not in giving a judgment, of whatsoever kind it may be, state that the accused is innocent or without guilt, but rather say that according to law nothing has been proved against him. Because when he later in the course of time once again is accused, and something then can be proved against him according to law, then he should be condemned without hindrance of a former verdict of not guilty."

The altruistic inquisitor, pious and good, condemns us each and all to be burnt at the stake for valid reasons with rational arguments. His consciousness is false and his rationality irrational.

My behaviour towards L in 1946, in regard to the blue envelope in 1953, and towards A, after seeing her eyes grow black inside the outline of the grey coat in 1963, can be logically defended. I am even convinced that I could have acted in no other way. (So be it. So is it written.) But if I have acted on a base of false consciousness, an ideological consciousness, then the guilt is on me. In that respect the long dead and by all men condemned Dominican friars were quite right; one can never declare oneself innocent, only for the time being be let off due to lack of evidence.

I had come to Oslo as a correspondent. It was difficult to obtain a visa. I had promised to write. I had credentials. I had been sitting at the East Railway Station in Oslo that whole first day. Listening to the footsteps of people passing. I wrote nothing.

There was an explosion in Oslo that autumn of 1945. I was walking the Möllergaten on my way to the Deichman library when the ground shook and the windows were smashed around me. Afterwards it was rumoured that it was sabotage. I was to write, but I didn't write and I fled. I had just become eighteen.

—You get hold of the news, you flee, you are worthless.

The lair. If it is at the Greenlandlejr between the meat hall and the debtor's prison or at Albogatan or at Fagervik is of no matter. When reality becomes too dubious you withdraw.

It must have been in October 1945 that my landlady came into my small rented room at the Greenlandlejr in Oslo. I lay on my bed with my feet up against the wall. Actually I had been standing on my head in my bed practising breathing techniques. I was interested in yoga. But as I heard her coming through the door I had noiselessly doubled up, folded myself like a clasp knife and now I was lying quietly with my legs stretched up against the flowered wallpaper. She talked. I said nothing. I had not

made my bed for three weeks. In the night I used to eat
ship biscuits. They were unrationed. When she had spoken
to me for half an hour without me answering—just lying
there and breathing regularly—she started to scream. Then
I understood that I must leave the lair. It wasn't enough
that I paid my rent. I also had to conform. Otherwise I
wouldn't be left in peace. Now I have a house of my own
(or owned by the bank), have also learnt to look as if I
do conform. You smile with your mouth and go through
the motions of conformity.

But I can still see my landlady. She was leaning down
over me and while she spoke her face got red. It started as
a flush on the cheeks. Then spread over her face. That interested me. She had eyes small as a pig's and these eyes
were staring at me. Her mouth was working the whole
time. At the corners of her mouth saliva collected and
formed drops. I didn't answer her, I said nothing, I didn't
move, I only breathed, and that I said nothing seemed to
upset her, the saliva began to froth. I was lying with my
feet propped up on the wall and I saw her face from under-
neath. This gave me a strange perspective on her:

—Man is an ugly animal, I thought, in twenty years'
time that is how you yourself will look.

There is this trapdoor in life. By opening the seemingly
smooth and unscalable walls I can now and then escape
the consequences by freezing myself in the state of on-
looking and immovability. I had already learned that as a
child. Because the important fact about my lying in that
unmade bed was not that I was lying but that I was looking on. It was a conflict of observation. A momentary and
for me—as for all of us—a not unusual paralyzation of the
ability to act.

The conflict between what the onlooker observes and
the possibility of changing the observed. The way the ob-

served seems to change as you (only) shift focus. The continuous struggle between the different observations sometimes leads to a situation of temporary balance as the forces counterbalance each other. Anxiety without action.

Of course I know that what I have written can (will) be misinterpreted. It is so easy to talk about neurosis and instinctive urges and inhibitions. But I repeat what I have said: reality is real and the anxiety is rational.

This escape into immovability is not unusual, it is not even specifically human. Most animals play dead. Now—twenty years later—I hope, though, that I in the future will act more often like a cornered rat and not like a cornered lizard. That is a very high aspiration. The highest, it seems.

Two weeks after the Second World War had ended in Europe I found Paracelsus. I had taken the night train to Gothenburg the day that peace was said to have broken out. In my berth I had been reading Marx: *The Poverty of Philosophy*. (Reason and rationality. Outlooking becoming insight leading to action changing the observed. A strong wine. I was drunk with happiness as the train rolled south through the night.)

Now, in Gothenburg, I rented a room and worked as a cub reporter. There Paracelsus found me. I might from the beginning say that it was not his mysticism that interested me, neither had I any illusions about his medical importance. It was the poet Paracelsus. I can see what I have underlined. Underlined with thick lines of red ink. (A young boy with blond hair, an underpaid newspaper apprentice who was supposed to exist on five dollars a week, but bought books, starved and sponged on Dag who had received food coupons from his mother. We ate one meal each every other day. In that way we both could use the coupons for the restaurant.)

Strike out the rest of this chapter. It concerns what a
young boy (JM) read, what he declaimed to a girl
one night near the sea; what he struggled to understand. When reading it I felt as if I betrayed him. He
was adolescent, he read and talked. But he believed
it. I make him ridiculous by showing him standing in
his (cheap, wartime) ersatz clothes at the sea, in front
of the girl, declaiming.

The chapter ended: with that background it will not be
difficult for the readers to understand why I had my feet
up against the wall and from below noticed how the face
of the landlady second by second was transformed into an
evil mask.

Which is a lie. No principle was lying there in the unmade bed. Only a scared teenager. I was eighteen and
scared.

When I had just come to Oslo I lived for some time at
a boardinghouse up at Majorstua. I have no longer any
clear memory of how long I lived there or the exact process
by which I left. (Which is an evasion—of course I could
remember if I tried. But it is of no consequence for this
story.) That was before I had got my room at the Greenlandlejr between the meat hall and the debtor's prison.

It was an old house. In all the rooms there was a smell
of mothballs, insect powder and carbolic acid. A smell of
poor students; brown furniture; long corridors.

In this house I found that I had got crab lice. It itched.
Suddenly I saw them. Small, ugly, flat animals. I got sick.
Hid. Cleaned up my vomit. Looked at myself in the mirror.

You remember how it was being eighteen? The fear of
syphilis. And then this, that the crab lice slowly crept up
into the armpits. After some weeks I even had them in my
eyebrows. I didn't dare to go to a doctor. I didn't want to

talk to anybody about the crab lice. I didn't even want to think about them. Lice!

I knew whom I had got them from, too. As I was leaving for Norway I had four girls going. I knew (or thought I knew) which one of them had given me the crab lice. What I found disgusting was the knowledge that I must have given the crab lice to the other three. Also I had met a girl in Oslo. I broke with her. I hid.

Yes, it was more or less like that. But the last sentences make the young JM too much of the lover. He was a normal eighteen-year-old. This is the way it was with the four girls and the crab lice. I had been working in Karlstad on the newspaper there. I had got to know a girl who was four years older—she was twenty-two; she was ashamed of being seen together with me who was only seventeen, so we only met in bed. It was good and nice and quite unromantic.

The day that the Nazis capitulated in Norway and Denmark there were big demonstrations in Stockholm. I walked beside a blond girl whom I had never seen before. We went hand in hand singing.

As I was taking the night train down to Gothenburg that evening in May 1945 when there was said to be peace in Europe, a girl followed me to the train. We talked; she kissed me. I had known her in the youth movement. Then the train left.

Staying in Stockholm for a week before going to Norway in August I met these girls again. I also met the girl I had been in love with the year before. Her eyes were green. The girl I had been walking with in the demonstration shared a room with the girl I had known from Karlstad. She worked in a dentist's office. The first night I went to bed with this girl instead of the one I

had known from Karlstad. Afterwards I climbed out of
the window—they had a room on the fourth floor above
Storgatan. There I let myself hang from the windowsill on my fingertips. Then I heaved myself up and made
a volte into the room. I was scared of falling, felt the
fingers slipping; but I used to do that. I never saw that
girl from the dentist's office again. But she gave me
crab lice.

The girl who had kissed me goodbye at the station I
met the next day. I followed her home and afterwards
she said:

—Going to bed is the only thing you care about.

I didn't know what to answer. I believe I gave her
crab lice. I have never asked. She continued to study,
she is a Member of Parliament now. A rather good one.
Specializing in social security. We meet now and then
at different public functions.

The girl I had known from Karlstad didn't like my
having gone to bed with her friend. She never took me
to their room again. We were together in the Djur-
gården, we lay under the oaks, and people were
stepping over us, I remember. It was a beautiful summer
night and afterwards we walked along the lake. I gave
her crab lice. That was the last time we were together.
Later on when I met her she always showed a strong
dislike for me.

I rang up the girl I had been in love with the year
before. We met in her parents' flat the day before I
left for Oslo. I liked her very much. Her parents were
on vacation. I stayed with her the whole night. She
promised to write me in Oslo. I gave her crab lice. She
never wrote.

My fear of doctors was not fear. It was shame. I knew
what they would say. I didn't want to hear them preach.

Many years later when I got gonorrhea for the first time and went to a clinic to get a penicillin injection and be rid of it, I had to listen to exactly those words I as an eighteen-year-old would not have stood for. But by then I had been able to toughen myself against the intrusiveness of others.

I tried to get rid of the crab lice by gasoline. But I nearly burnt up my genitals. The crab lice survived. When the lice had reached my eyebrows and I was walking around with sunglasses so that nobody could see the colonies of small grey lice that were crawling above my eyes, I moved into my room at the Greenlandlejr. I locked myself in and shaved my whole body. The crab lice didn't go into the head hair so I didn't have to shave my head. But I kept on shaving eyebrows and armpits and genitals until every louse and every egg was gone. During that time I didn't go out.

That is why I was lying in bed when my landlady came.

The fear of syphilis haunted me for many years. Like many teenagers before me and after me I studied my body and worried about sores. As soon as I had got rid of the crab lice I started to have my blood checked. As I had a strong distaste for going to a doctor to ask for an examination and as I at the same time had very little money, I got the examination by selling blood to different hospitals. I got food (meat) and beer and some crowns. Before they took blood from me they asked:

—Venereal diseases?

—How would I know? I answered.

Then they checked me. They made a Wassermann test before they accepted me as a blood donor. In this way I by and by became convinced that I didn't have syphilis.

The difficulty in remembering: I gave blood. I sold blood. I was very poor. That can be described. But why did I sell blood? Because I was poor and got food (real meat) and beer and money? A pint of my blood would keep me going for nearly a week. Or was the reason more psychological? Studying my body for syphilis sores I went to the hospital—well knowing that they never accept blood without testing for syphilis if the donor seems suspect; I seemed very suspect—and sold blood? The description can never rest on any one of these two reasons. Both are valid. But if I described myself as poor, selling blood, eating a piece of meat—then the reader could feel pity. Could like. Poverty is always likeable (in others). If I described myself as selling blood because of fear of syphilis and unwillingness to go for a normal (that is, free of charge and rather brutal) checkup together with all the people the police round up (the rich have their private doctors), then it would be a social description. If I just said that selling blood was an easy and profitable way of checking if I had syphilis, then the reader would dislike me. His own fear of syphilis would override his rational knowledge that the blood of donors is checked. Always necessary to go one step further.

The reason that I was lying there on an unmade bed inside the darkness with the blinds down and the curtains closed and training myself in yoga and breathing techniques can thus be sought on different levels of consciousness. The answers consequently become different.

It should now be said that this whole picture of my situation in the autumn of 1945 is thoroughly false. False though not a word is a lie. Because I left the most important unsaid.

I had always spoken about writing. I "felt so much" and had "so much to say." But only in my lair at the Greenlandlejr did I start writing the first pieces I could accept. A thin volume of poetry and prose poetry: *Puberty*. I still accept it. All other manuscripts from the period up to 1955 I have burned. But this thin little book that I wrote in a mixture of fear and revolt sitting in my dark room while the crab lice were crawling up my eyebrows I still want to publish at a suitable moment.

That it could not be published at that time had a very special reason. The publisher wrote me a long letter—two pages—long and kind. It talked of "intensity and passion" and other nice things but ended:

". . . I believe mainly that if your little book was published it would, in the hands of ruthless enemies, be used against your parents in a very dangerous manner. If another publisher should prove himself willing to publish your book with a content more or less the one that it now has, then the manuscript ought first to be submitted to and approved by your parents. I hope you don't mind my saying this."

No, I didn't mind. I had expected nothing else. My father was at that time a member of a very disputed government. My small book would possibly have led to a new and intensified morality debate. It was generally agreed that the best I could do for the labour movement and the country was to shut up and disappear, as far away as possible. I found it a little bit difficult to accept this line of thought but understood that there was not much I could do about it. For a while I thought of staying in Norway. Sigurd Hoel, the writer, wrote a nice letter to me about my manuscript. Stenersen gave me a grant and said that I was a new Rimbaud. But I didn't believe that very much. So I went on. But in leaving I took my manuscript along. It still is there—in yellow cover—in the top drawer of my desk.

At that time I was eighteen. I still had illusions. I didn't know that that letter was to cost me ten years. The publishers had discussed the question. They went to the same dinner parties, they were friends of friends. They belonged to the same group as my parents. Nice, honest people of moderately radical opinion. For ten years I had only the most impressive collection of refusals in the country to show as proof of my existence. In Gothenburg I made a wallpaper of them. Pasted them on the wall of my room in the attic. I and my friends (B was one then) laughed. The arguments from 1945 came back time after time. The government remained the same albeit my father had left for Geneva and the UN. In 1949 I got a letter with the letterhead "KANSLIHUSET," the government chancellery. The writer stated that a publisher had submitted one of my novels to him and he expressed his disgust. And the well-known writers were friends of friends too. Now many years later—when I publish some of the things that were turned down then—they come up to me, smile, hold their martinis, very dry, in their hands and say:

—I am sorry. I had that manuscript to read many years ago. But as everybody said you were impossible I never really read it.

There was only one single writer in the whole of Sweden who gave me any support. That was Erik Blomberg.

But in one way this helped me. I knew what I wanted to say and I began to understand why I didn't like what the others were writing. But of course I have never forgotten and forgiven nothing. I would rather fry in hell than stretch out my little finger to help any of those men and women who for ten years stopped even the possibility of my publishing an article under my own name.

When they smile at me I do not smile back. I have wished them dead since 1945 and I do so still.

That was my greatest personal defeat. I can still feel the smell of hunger and dirt, and crab lice, and dreams from that autumn. I thought of emigrating to the USA because there was no place for me in Sweden. But I had taken part in the demonstrations in 1945, was eighteen and considered subversive. Anyway, I could get no recommendation. I was young, I considered myself (still do) a socialist. Believing then in a very naive and pure-hearted way not only in the goals of the labour movement but also in its organization. I could not understand why these people (and their good and liberal bourgeois friends) suddenly began to consider this eighteen-year-old a political danger. But all the politicians in the labour movement—from Per Albin Hansson, the prime minister and chairman of the Social Democratic party, who sent me the greeting that I ought to learn to keep my damn trap shut, after I had managed to get a short article about socialism published in a youth paper, to local Communist big shots in Gothenburg —agreed that the best thing I could do for the labour movement and the country was to disappear. That the most well-known and liberal bourgeois publishers then repeated the same thing was the final condemnation.

I kept these letters. Today the letter writers do not like to be reminded of what they have written. But I have always enjoyed reading these letters again when the letter writers stand up and speak for the freedom of literature whenever a writer in the Soviet Union or eastern Europe or Spain, for the same tactical and political reasons, has been silenced. I can't really see the difference (as long as the writers that have been silenced are not outrightly killed or jailed but only silenced) and thus I have not

been able to admit that these Swedish lovers of literary
freedom have any right to talk.

It would be wrong if the reader read this as only an
interesting detail in the life of JM. It concerns the very
root of the question about loyalty, ideas and organized
ideas. In my case the situation was complicated by
"family considerations"; but I can't accept that it is re-
duced to the family level and becomes sort of an en-
larged Oedipus story.

About the role of my parents in this, I know very
little. We rarely saw each other. I never met their
friends after I was ten. I believe that they in a general way agreed with the political necessity to keep
me quiet. Because if what I wrote could hurt their
work . . . *if* they thought that and if they considered
their work important, it would have been rational to
want me quiet. But I don't think they did anything
about it. It would have been unpleasant. One doesn't
do things like that to children. I think it was much
simpler than that. They sat at evenings and talked
to dear friends about me—that is, spoke of their love
or something. The friends then went out and did the
work and no one was to blame.

It would be so simple to escape by making the problem private (Paracelsus: faith or article of faith). At
a rather early stage I was in this way forced to make
myself unpleasantly conscious of the conflict between
the idea and the organized idea; the religion and its
church; the theory and its party; I was forced to make
a choice. What really was demanded of me was that I
should deny myself completely; deny what I had seen
and what I had experienced and what I thought; deny

what I—like most of my generation—felt for the established politicians during the war; deny what we thought about the traitorous behaviour of the representatives from all the major parties. In Sweden, as in Denmark, they wouldn't have minded an occupation as long as it didn't influence their salaries. This was demanded of me, not by my parents for familial reasons—had that been so then I could have saved the situation easily by a private revolt—but by all the representatives of the society, party functionaries, and editors. And the demand was made in the name of the higher interest. Socialism, the future, all that I believe to be right, demanded that I either conform or at least announce that I had become a liberal or a conservative. But I could neither conform to the party tactics nor announce that I was not a socialist.

In that situation I advised my friend L to hang himself. For myself I kept on living.

Today, 1968, I have been convinced for a long time that it is the idea and not the organized idea that has any rights over me. And as I managed to survive these years after 1945 I can feel rather sure that I will—as long as I don't acquire friends—keep my integrity. Be able to work.

It was all so very simple. I was of no importance. A kid. But I had a loud voice and I tried to make myself heard. As what I tried to say both about politics and about morals was considered to be stupid, but at the same time could lose some votes for the labour movement, it was of course necessary to shut me up. As for my parents and their work, I did—and do—consider some of it valuable and correct. But I did—and do— also consider much of it meaningless because it does not change society. That was exactly what I was not sup-

posed to say about their and their friends' work. Now—
a generation later—it is quite clear that I was right and
they were wrong. Their work was rational and reasonable and good—but it did not reach the goals they had
set. The social situation remained unchanged. And the
new generation that now is growing up consequently
throws these tactics and this style of work from the
1930s in the dustbin. Of course, I did not speak about
my parents. I didn't for two reasons. One was that I
did not like being private and the second was that I did
not want people to say that I reacted in a private manner. But it is evident that I drew my conclusions about
the leaders of the Swedish labour movement and their
tactics from having seen them as a child in my home. I
sat quietly listening, was patted on the head, ate my
cake and drank my milk, and kept my thoughts to myself. When I tried to utter them it suddenly became a
political necessity to get me to shut up. Up to now I
have not made that personal background public.

As I left Oslo Nic said:
—Don't worry, Jan. You are like a cat. You will always
land on your feet. You will manage. You will manage
despite them all.
That was in 1946. She was the only one I had ever
trusted. She kept her integrity until she died. When she at
last was to get her responsible position—the one for which
she had been qualified for so many years—and people
told her to be sensible and keep quiet and not speak
against Norway signing the NATO agreements, then she
journeyed up and down the country speaking against it.
Of course they took the post from her immediately and
gave it to another—and less qualified.
—I knew they would, she said. But that is no reason to
be silent.

When they told her to be reasonable, she said what was reasonable and true and got many enemies.

She also gave me advice that I as yet have had no reason to follow. "It is not so dangerous to be tortured as you believe. It is your fear of torture that is dangerous. Learn to relax. Nobody can reach you if you don't let them. The torturers win over you as long as you hope and struggle. Just give up and relax and shut off." She spoke from experience.

That experience she shares with many of our contemporaries. During the last generation it has become quite evident that the monuments our Western ideals construct rest on a firm base of torn-off fingernails.

In this chapter I have struck out a whole series of stories. They all concerned torture, false confessions, terror, murder, lies. I struck them out because I wanted to keep the writing personal. I could easily escape my guilt by saying that we all share and share alike that guilt. Still I take it for granted that my readers remember what has been done. That they remember everything: the final solution of the Jewish question; the Stalin era, the Churchill decision to bomb the civilians, the colonial wars for plunder and freedom (with chopped-off heads in Malaya, electrodes against the genitals in Algeria, napalm in Vietnam), OAS, the lying politicians, everything. But I want to underline that it has been the European, the Western intellectuals that have led and fulfilled these actions in every phase. We have written the theories, we have filled the universities with learned men giving rational motivations and reasonable techniques for every crime. And in every new betrayal we have always been able to supply the demand for hangmen.

And everything that has been done has been done

with the most sincere desire to carry on the struggle for
our ideals. This has been the century of the European
intelligentsia.

SUMMA

Only by a hairsbreadth did I escape taking the road of
art by painting an apocalypse which—even if true
—by making the guilt general, by making it a "human
condition" (or at least a "European burden"), lets each
single one of us disappear out of the picture.

Few burdens are so easy to carry as original sin or collective guilt. Storytelling is a danger and fictionalizing is
a temptation to be avoided. Art lies with form.

What I have written up to now has been honest. It has
not been directly false. Like all private honesty and personal apology, it has been without honour.

Honesty is not costly. Baring one's life is as simple and
as unemotional as baring one's body. I don't know anything that I would not—after a rapidly passing uneasiness
—be able to say about JM and his private life.

But what I have written gives only the patterns and not
the explanation for those actions that—however I turn
and twist the sequence of events and however I peel my
actions like I peel an onion and however I choose my
words and carefully handle the interpretations—must be
experienced as guilty. The guilt was not lack of consciousness. But the conscious inactivity.

A didn't phone me just to take me out for a meal. She
also wanted to talk about what had happened to her at

the Social Security Board. She gave an account of her discussion with the social worker. And I had arranged for her to go to that large grey building near the freight yard in Stockholm.

A meant nothing for me and my life as long as she was alive. But I understood early that she was in a deep crisis. She was marked by death. Some weeks before the telephone call that was to be my last contact with A, I had become convinced that she shortly would make a serious attempt to commit suicide.

There were no direct reasons for me to believe this. She had not told me anything that could give that impression. But I knew a little about her background, I knew some of her personal problems, and that taken together with the impression she gave as a being (the direct and intuitive way in which you grasp the personality of another through the voice, the gestures, the way the eyes move, the pattern of movement) quite convinced me that she shortly would make a successful attempt at suicide. I said nothing of this to A. But I spoke to Gun about it.

I had lent A my flat. By this I felt I had intervened in her life and taken her responsibility upon me. I had warned her that she had to keep herself hard against all those people who were going to try to get her out of the flat. In a housing shortage as great as that of Stockholm people become like hungry beasts. When there has been a shortage of housing for twenty years then there is nothing so low or so brutish that an ordinary citizen will abstain from doing it if that deed will give him a flat in the centre of the town without his having to go to prison for it. I assumed, though, that she was unable to be hard. She was too weak to be able to keep her grasp on the flat when the others, the neighbours and friends, would claw and struggle to get it. But it was necessary for her to have a flat. Somebody had to protect her rights. If she only had somewhere to live, a room that would be her own and where she could live without being hunted and without being afraid that somebody suddenly would throw the door open and scream, "Out! Out!" then she would be able to solve her problems. She had all the possibilities. She was young, she was intelligent, she was pretty—nearly beautiful—she knew a lot and she had work. She was in no way criminal. If she had been that, if she had been a prostitute for example, then she would have been saved. She would have had the gang, or at least the pimp, she would have had some kind of security. She needed companionship and security. She was like that.

Therefore I called T, the doctor of social medicine who was in charge of the grey house. I had known him for a long time. He had been one of the first who told me not to continue writing when I was young. He was well known in Sweden both for his work and for his activity in the service of all good causes imaginable. But he had power and power to help and this girl did not need anything extraordinary. He also proved himself helpful when I telephoned. But he showed that he found me overwrought and excited when I told him that she was going to commit suicide.

—Young girls often say that.

—She hasn't said anything about it.

—Well?

Intuition is not an argument you are able to use in this society.

T arranged for me to talk to the social worker. She listened in a friendly way to what I had to say. But she too found my interest in the case strange. It seemed she suspected that I had made A pregnant and could not arrange a nice and tidy semilegal abortion but had to leave A to them. This irritated me. But I was careful not

to let my irritation show. I knew how these people react.
You have to smile pleasantly to them and laugh at their
jokes to get them to work.

Then I coaxed A. Spoke to her about her need for a flat.
She could live in my flat. But the landlord would try to get
rid of her. He had a slight legal chance—if he could prove
that I was subletting he could get an eviction order. He
was using this. He was a member of the Landlords Association and they had some of the best lawyers in town. I had
tried to talk to him. After all the flat was just a single room.
But he didn't talk to me. He only corresponded through
lawyers. I knew that there was a fair chance for A to keep
the flat if she was hard as stone. If she never opened the
door except for people she knew well, if she never talked
on the telephone without being conscious that the landlord and his lawyers would try to phone her up and get her
to say something that could be used against her in the case.
They had permission to use tape recorders. But she was
not the type of person who could live in this fashion which
is normal in a civilized society. So I coaxed her. There is a
welfare state around somewhere. They speak about it at
election time. She paid her taxes. She had the same rights
as others. She had the right to get assistance. Every politician in the country was saying this. A didn't want to go
to the authorities.

—I haven't done anything wrong, she said.

But I spoke convincingly about the state and the society
existing for the protection and care of the citizens and that
the officials get paid by tax money in order to work and be
helpful. (For myself I don't believe this, but the argument
can be used if you want something done. After all, it is
what they all say.)

A spoke to the social worker and they had a nice chat.
Unfortunately the case was difficult to solve. A was not
criminal. A was not moronic. A was not a prostitute. A was

not even drifting. She had work and she went to her work every day at nine o'clock and those days that she didn't work overtime she left her work at five. She had temporary lodgings. The only strange thing about her was that she read poetry. But that was not reason enough for the state to intervene. The social worker promised, though, to keep her in mind and see if something happened that would make it possible for her to help A.

A phoned me to tell this. And I was furious at her. I knew how nice and calm she had been. I knew how reasonable she had been and how calmly she had let herself be convinced that there was nothing the social worker could do. And I knew that she had smiled pleasantly when she said goodbye. When I spoke to the social worker afterwards it was quite evident that she thought that what JM had said about A and suicide proved more that JM was unsound than that A needed help.

It irritated me that A had given up so easily. She ought to have understood that the social worker would say all this. The social worker didn't want to work unnecessarily or give away a room in one of the municipal boarding-houses so easily. I had told A how the social worker would first talk about the impossibility—but that if A just kept on she would get a place to live. But I also understood that A couldn't help being soft and weak. And I didn't show A that I was furious or irritated. (Didn't I?)

In defence of the social worker and the authorities I ought to say though that if the state had to take responsibility for all the young people that are without homes and without housing and without protection or any form of defence, and if the state would do something before the "cases" became criminal or prostitutes or alcoholics, then Sweden would be as beautiful as an election speech. But not even the politicians are lying. I know them. I have seen them closely. In winter Stockholm is a chilly place to sleep in if you sleep under a bridge. None of the thousands who have to do that ever becomes a politician. Few survive. I had luck. I survived. But to the politicians—from all parties—all this is just a row of figures in the social statistics. Because in order to be a politician you need a settled background and when you become a politician you get a better flat. How could they then help believing their election speeches?

The social worker really did more for A than the rules permitted just by talking to her. She is not salaried in order to spend her time talking to just anybody who wants to talk.

So A committed suicide.

But this way of presenting the facts transfers the guilt from me to—the more abstract entity—society in general. As this society exists objectively and functions as it does according to historical development and social laws (that can be studied), the guilt changes; first to a general responsibility (the responsibility for this tragic development, etc., etc., etc.) and then to historical inevitability (fate, to use an older and better word). This makes it possible for JM to indulge in sentiment and emotion without any danger. A is dead. History moves onward. Time marches. JM condemns; then goes to sleep. That is of course a very false way of escaping. We shan't let JM get away so easily.

As I spoke so emotionally about "society" with what right did I trust "the authorities"? How could I assume that they would have, could have, wanted to have any form of understanding for A when I never found that understanding for myself? And how can I at the same time write about what was done to me when I was very young (and write with feeling) and gladly hand over A (so much weaker, with so little of that catlike ability to always land on her feet) to the same people and expect them to help her?

For myself I strove to keep away from them during my youth as I knew that they would—that is what they are salaried for—try to adjust me. The authorities have police and courts and doctors and reformatories; but how could I assume that they would also show responsibility?

My guilt was not that I drove her to suicide. I didn't. My influence on her was very small. I never discussed the question with her. And I never let her see what I thought and believed about her. It might be possible that I in one way or another—a gesture, an expression of the eyes, an intonation—betrayed my thoughts; but I find it unbelievable that this could have pushed her to death.

If I wanted to I could make literature out of that. A reasonably good chapter. Emotions, gestures, small revealing details, intuition. But not at this stage. That was done some pages ago. Lied with form.

I didn't play any role in her life except as a fellow human she met by chance; someone who lent her a flat. Of course I understand that the reader might have got a different impression—as did the doctor—since I have told about the way in which I speculated on her. The only thing I can say about that is that I wonder about and speculate upon all the people I come into touch with. That is a part of my work—and at the same time one of the reasons why I limit my contacts. Because they interest me I have to isolate myself.

My guilt is that I was conscious enough to see what was going on, that I began to act, but did not carry my action through to the end. My guilt is that of the consciousness that does not carry responsibility.

I can't discuss whether I am guilty or not. My guilt is evident. I would have been without guilt if I had been lacking in consciousness about her situation. But I was conscious. Conscious enough to talk to doctors and social workers. Conscious enough to take up a fight with the landlord and struggle with him and the Landlords Association. If I had been unsuccessful, been beaten in this struggle, then I would have been without guilt. I could honestly have said that I did all I could do. This I cannot say.

Knowing but not doing is betrayal, carries guilt. Why did I then betray? And why have we that have been the bearers of consciousness always betrayed? Let that be which we knew would be?

I had promised to write an essay on folk music. On the lyrics of this music as literature. It was spring. The spring of 1963. I was sitting on the floor of my study in front of the record player. I selected different records. Taped some of them, made notes, marked interesting phrases. The amplifier was turned up to high volume; the doors to the garden were open and I felt like I was sitting in a balloon of sound.

I had been working like this for three days. I had collected a nice little heap of notes. I like music, I like folk songs. But I was beginning to feel uncomfortable with this work. During the ages people have been hungry, betrayed, wretched; they have been killed off in wars, kicked by their superiors, struck by epidemics; they have seen their nearest die, seen their homes burned down, seen their superiors ride past. Out of this they have made tales and music and poetry. Some of this—what still existed—has

been recorded and collected. This is good. Some of it is
still sung and played. The blues for instance. But where?
for whom?

Art serves. Agreed. But whom does it serve? It doesn't
matter if the singer stands in a night club or a concert
hall. The audience is the same. Upper and upper-middle
class. To sing for them is art. Is a betrayal. They have been
the ones who have gained the whole time. Then you also
serve them the screams of their victims. That is art.

Even writing seriously about the lyrics became disgusting. I was sitting in this balloon of sound thinking about
this. I had promised to write this essay. I knew the editors. Good people. But for whom was I really performing?
In another time, in another age, possibly.

But not now. My promise was a promise but it would be
a betrayal to keep it. I had seen the well-known public
figures, the status bearers, the big progressive writers and
artists passing the continents. And for whom? Jesters and
trained monkeys performing for the masters.

And how get out of this? How write so the words are
unusable for the masters but are still written in such a
way that they will be printed. (To be honest and un-
printable is no victory. Words exist only when they are
read.)

Suddenly I shut off the loudspeakers. Telephoned to
Stockholm and tried to find A. She was not at her job. She
didn't answer the telephone. I sent her a cable. Asked her
to get in touch with me immediately.

As I put the receiver down I remembered my quarrel
with Nic in Paris in 1955. That was the last time I saw her.
I had given her the four Bessie Smith LP's that Philips
had just released. We quarrelled about "Long Old Road."
The words: "You can't trust nobody/you might as well be
alone."

—You have to trust, she said.

I meant that you can't trust anybody anyway, so . . .
She spoke about the deep need for trust.
—Now she is dead, I thought.
I looked through my notes, put them in order, and wondered what and if I should write. But all the time, anxiety
and restlessness. Phoned A. Nobody answered, the phone
just kept on ringing far away.

The next day I phoned the office where she worked and
then the janitor. As I talked to him they had just found
her. I spoke with the police before they had even carried
her out of my kitchen.

And this it was difficult for me to explain to them: that
I had been sitting seventy kilometres away and knew that
she was dead.

When the last call was finished I put down the receiver,
collected my notes on folk music and put them in the box
for unfinished work. That essay will never be written.

Now A was dead and I had been expecting that for a
long time. And I could have prevented it. But I did not
prevent. As I put the receiver down and put my notes away
I did this in the awareness of my complete and final betrayal.

There were many practical reasons why I did nothing.
There was no time. There was much else that had to be
done. Articles that had to be written. Proofs corrected.
(The very language of these sentences is the language of
defeat. By not saying: "I wanted to write articles" but
"Articles had to be written" I fling off my responsibility.)
It was true I was short of money, my debts were large
and I had to work hard.

And I was worried. I had a great deal of trouble finding
a way out. I had just returned after five years in Asia. I
had no longer any belief whatsoever in what I had more

or less consciously believed before—that anything good
could come from Europe, the Europeans (in the sense
"Western" not as a geographical predetermination, of
course). I did not know how to work. To describe was
always honest . . . but I had a gnawing suspicion that all
my words would be used by others for other ends. For
Western ends.

What we were doing to Asia, I had seen.

But this is no excuse. Nearly no explanation. I have
demanded only one thing of myself. What I do should be
done consciously and deliberately. The excuses I have
made are those excuses I have always found despicable
in others. If I had been able to say that I consciously decided that A was of little importance and that I had to
demand a concentrated effort of myself in my work and
this concentration demanded that I let A be sacrificed,
then I would have acted consciously. (The validity of the
reasoning could of course be discussed.) But I cannot say
that there was any such conscious decision.

I let A die out of fruitless inactivity. Despite my knowledge.

Thus the story about the death of A is in reality the
story of the Western intellectual. As I betrayed A, so have
we always betrayed. Because the unconscious one does not
betray. He walks secure through life. But we who are a
part of the tradition—the Europeans—and who carry on
the tradition we have betrayed with awareness, insight
and consciousness, we have carefully analyzed all the wars
before they were declared. But we did not stop them.
(And many amongst us became the propagandists of the
wars as soon as they were declared.) We describe how the
poor are plundered by the rich. We live among the rich.
Live on the plunder and pander ideas to the rich. We have
described the torture and we have put our names under

appeals against torture, but we did not stop it. (And we ourselves became torturers when the higher interests demanded torture and we became the ideologists of torture.) Now we once more can analyze the world situation and describe the wars and explain why the many are poor and hungry. But we do no more.

We are not the bearers of consciousness. We are the whores of reason.

□

NEW MORNINGS
FOR OLD

A has been dead a long time now. The house where she died was torn down twenty years ago. There are blocks of new office buildings in that area. The town plan is new. The kitchen where she died would float in the air thirty feet above the pavement now. Few remember her. I begin to have difficulty recalling her face. Sometimes I don't even think of her for weeks at a time. But when I do see her she is still very young.

And now when nearly thirty years have passed another generation has been forced to consciousness as the fake socialism of the Russian Empire crumbles, the Cold War fades away and a victorious Greater Germany appears having won the peace in Europe as Japan did in Asia. Do I still consider the intellectuals the whores of reason?

I do. That is why I am sitting here with the forest behind me and the lake in front of me writing about the Five Years of Freedom in France from the revolution in July 1830 to the new censorship laws in September 1835. Writing about our contemporaries, the European intellectuals of that time one hundred and sixty years ago. The young revolutionaries who fought for Liberty and woke up a year later to find that they had established the reign of the bankers. Theirs was for a couple of years a heroic fight in the streets and in that press the officials then called subversive. In 1835 it was all over.

Some of these young revolutionary intellectuals became bankers themselves a generation later in the service of Napoleon III; many among them like Philipon and Balzac were to dominate the official media during the decades to come; and some of the heroes of 1830 lost their foothold on reality when the ideals crashed. Like poor Peytel who tumbled and fell and was beheaded in 1839.

But 1835 was not the end of the story.

Every generation these hundred and sixty years has gone through nearly the same experience. Nearly, because every time we are blown a little bit forward with the wind of change we have generated.

This book took more than six years to write. It was written during such a change and became part of the change.

And looking back I see the India-bound 4,000 ton cargo liner M/S Bengal rolling from side to side.

She heaved up and then sat shuddering in the storm that was sweeping the Bay of Biscay in January 1961. I can see the bleak bluish light in the corridor. There is frothy water swishing past my feet. It has leaked in from the deck. I hold on to the brass handrail as the ship plunges. She was built at the end of the War, it is her last trip under Swedish flag on this route to the East and I hear the metal creaking around me. There is a cold, wet draft on my face and as I open the cabin door I see a younger Jan Myrdal writing. He has a wet towel on the desk to keep his small Olivetti typewriter from sliding off. He writes with two fingers as a writer should and as he has done since he became a cub reporter in Karlstad seventeen years earlier and he now writes in pace with the ship; as she rolls to the left he quickly pounds out a line and as she heaves he steadies the machine with his left hand and continues to write with just one finger and then as she rolls to the right and the carriage returns on its own he sits back and formulates the next line.

Gun and I were the only passengers aboard the M/S Bengal bound for Bombay. She was built for the Scandinavian South Asia trade according to prewar specifications to carry goods and missionaries. Now the trade pattern had

changed, the missionaries were flying and she was going to
be sold to Hong Kong. We were on our way back to India
after coming from Central Asia over Sverdlovsk to Stockholm where we had stayed for some weeks. Gun had held
an exhibition of paintings, I had published my book on Afghanistan. We had money to keep us going for a year at
least. There were still some dollars left from 1959 when we
worked with a foundation in California (Peace through Understanding) making audiovisual education kits on Iran, Afghanistan and Central Asia for schools in the United States.
Gun had sold rather well at the exhibition. The book on Afghanistan was being printed in a second edition. I had got a
literary grant; the cooperative weekly *Vi* wanted articles
from Burma and had promised to grubstake us for another
year when and if we got our visa for China.

I wanted to go back to India also because I wanted to finish the book on India I had begun in 1958. I didn't know
then that I would leave India a year later without having
finished the book; that in fact it would take nearly twenty
more years to finish. But when the captain of the M/S
Bengal asked me about India I replied by quoting Ibn Ba-
tuta: "The wall that surrounds Delhi has no equal," because we had already spent two years in India and I knew
that I knew nearly nothing. But that I wanted to know.

Yesterday, as we were two days out of Rotterdam I had
started writing the first draft of what would become a chapter in this book. I had slept deeply the first night out after
drinking Russian champagne with the captain talking of India and the Far East and the convoys during the last war.
The captain was only two years older, he was from the
Swedish West Coast and this was the first ship of his own.
The former captain had left him a store room full of Cri-
mean champagne. I had woken up late in my bunk, felt the
movement of the ship and the last lines of a long argument
on Villon I had dreamed were still ringing in my ears:

—In the thirty-fourth year of my life not quite sane and not quite mad I will settle this ledger of personal accounts. I have liked François Villon from the very first time I read him as a boy. There was a very good Swedish translation of his Testament that I got 1941 playing dice in the school year during the noon break. I won it from Sten Ljung, a friend of mine at Bromma High School who we said was to—and he could have but he did not—become the great painter in our generation. His father was a good scholar. He not only talked of Villon, he used to sing for us boys in Latin and German out of the Carmina Burana, the collection of thirteenth century Goliard songs. He had a great library. Much of it still is mine. Mainly won from Sten at the poker games near the coal bin in the school basement when we were thirteen, fourteen in 1941. Rousseau, Diderot, E.T.A. Hoffman. Sometimes I lost though. I lost my bike and a radio. That was a little difficult to explain at home. But I managed. The janitor never caught us and in 1942 we didn't play either dice or poker any longer.

I would have said then—and I say now—that Villon was a contemporary European intellectual for better or worse. And in this dream 1961 I felt suddenly very happy when I heard the words:

—Not quite sane and not quite mad I will settle this ledger of personal accounts.

I had switched the order of sane and mad in Villon's sentence and I had left out the line that I could hear Helge Ljung recite: Que toutes mes hontes j'eus beues—having drunk my fill of shame. That could come later I thought. I woke Gun and recited all the first three opening verses of the Testament in Swedish. But as I stood up I still felt some of the champagne in my knees and I could not remember in what language I had been formulating in my dream. It sounded like French and I would have like to have done it in French: En l'an trentequatrième de mon âge/Ne du tout

sage, ne du tout fol...But I would not have been able to
finish it in that language. Anyway I told Gun about it:

—I am now going to write a ledger of personal accounts.

I then went looking for the captain and when I found
him at breakfast I told him I needed somewhere to sit and
write, and as there were no other passengers he gave me an
empty cabin to work in.

I stand there in that spare cabin of the M/S Bengal in
January 1961 looking over his shoulder at what Jan Myrdal
writes. He has not begun to get bald at the top of his head
yet. He is talking as he writes. He often does. Tasting the
words. I hear him and remember that he started to write in
Swedish. As he takes the paper out of the typewriter I can
read the last line: "...and found that most of them had
never realized that the earth is round." But what he starts
typing on the new page I can't read clearly. The whole picture becomes dim and goes silent; thirty years away now
the words become blurred. And I know they were to be
many times rewritten until six and a half years later; at
06:35 one morning in the summer of 1967 in Havana in
Cuba I wrote—in English this time, but on the same small
Olivetti—the last words and the book was finished:

> Now we once more can analyze the world situation
> and describe the wars and explain why the many are
> poor and hungry. But we do no more.
>
> We are not the bearers of consciousness. We are the
> whores of reason.

Yes, the text has a history. That history is both personal
and general. Let me be honest. A writer is no innocent.
There was a theoretical background. From the very beginning I didn't aim at writing just a saleable ledger of personal accounts for the Xmas sale. A book where I would
add up the feelings, the affectations and defects of a Swed-

ish writer during the postwar years. Instead I wanted to get past the defense mechanisms of the reader by telling stories. And by telling the stories seemingly at random and using my own life as raw material the text would help the reader to become conscious. Not really at random of course; there was to be a structure. (The dice are loaded!) But a structure that was overdetermined and not planned.

In doing this I thought I would myself become more conscious of both the age of my times—as Paracelsus would have said—and the determining forces in my life. You can't step into the same river twice and beginning to write a novel you know that the same writer will not step out of it. It is easy to see the outlines of such as Marx and Freud—and Reich—behind these words and this discussion of the role of conscious living. That is not surprising. These are ideas of my time and my environment in Europe. I grew up with Marx and Freud. They made it possible for me to see the reality behind the masks and the roles being played.

For different reasons—growing up in several countries with contradictory sets of morals, manners and beliefs and thus getting a multilayered pattern of behavior; then as Hitler seemed victorious I was a young teenager sitting in the encircled Sweden (a sort of Northern Vichy) reading Marx and Freud. I managed not to keep in step. When I began publishing novels the critics had difficulty in placing me. Some just hated—"There ought to be a bounty for shooting him," wrote the Catholic critic Sven Stolpe about my first novel. And editorialists in leading liberal papers quoted him and agreed. "Bounty"... it sounds even harsher in Swedish: "skottpengar på honom." I have never heard of anybody else in Sweden getting that type of criticism. But I really didn't mind. Nic had visited Reich in the United States and sent me his *Listen, Little Man.* I liked it. I still do. Stolpe and the others behaved just as Wilhelm Reich had said that they would.

And whatever they wrote I knew that the novel was not too bad as first novels go. No masterpiece maybe but still it later got translated to different languages. They are still printing new editions of it in Sweden. And in the main the critics calmed down. I was even getting grants. Both my latest novel and the book on Afghanistan got good reviews. In 1961 I had no reason to complain.

Politically Sweden was still an intellectual deep-freeze. A year earlier Harold Macmillan had spoken of the Wind of Change. "And whether we like it or not this growth of national consciousness is a political fact." But when I, just before boarding the train to Rotterdam and the M/S Bengal, had paraphrased him and spoken on the Swedish Radio of the real World Revolution that was changing South America, Africa and Asia; how the empires were tumbling and their ideologies of racism and Western supremacy were being torn down the leading liberal newspaper in Sweden, the *New York Times* of Stockholm, *Dagens Nyheter* demanded that the producer responsible for letting Jan Myrdal talk should be fired from the state radio. *Dagens Nyheter* had also found my book on Afghanistan suspect; what I had written on the British wars in Afghanistan seemed to them "anti-Western." The editors of *Dagens Nyheter* were—and remain!—the most vigilant liberal gatekeepers seeing to it that news not fit to be printed should never reach Swedish eyes.

The Ledger of Personal Accounts I was writing aboard M/S Bengal was an attempt to circumvent these gatekeepers. I kept on writing and publishing parts of it now and then during the coming years.

Then during the spring of 1967 Gun Kessle and I had been working in Cambodia for the book "Angkor and the Art of Imperialism."

The Cultural Revolution was in full swing in China. There were peasant revolts in Battambang west of where we were working. The United States was launching an offensive in "War Zone C" with 25,000 troops. Across the border the villages were being burned down, people were fighting for their lives. But here in Angkor Gun Kessle and I were strolling from monument to monument discussing the ornaments of the ninth century and the building techniques of the tenth century. This could be described as the normal behavior of petit-bourgeois intellectuals. But in my introduction to the book of Gun Kessle's photographs from Angkor I explained how I saw this intellectual work:

> The discussion of ninth-century ornaments is also a part of the necessary struggle against imperialism.
>
> This rotten society of ours is kept up by its dividing walls. Here a cell for revolt, there a cell for art; here a space for literature, there a space for economics—between them the walls. But these walls are load-bearing. The walls are the structure of this society. To raze them is part of the struggle for liberation.
>
> You stand face to face with the stones of Angkor. Beyond a border there is a war. But when you yourself face this stone then "beauty" becomes a concrete reality. These faces of stone were hewn by sweating men in a bloody time of repression and revolt.
>
> To write about Jayawarman VII and get beaten up by the cops; to stand in the midst of the dirt and violence writing fiction; to collect money for the striking mineworkers and lecture on Strindberg; to publish the secret Swedish army regulations on the use of gas against "rioting" strikers and to demand back all of history and all the millennia—that is to take part in the razing of the load-bearing walls of imperialism.
>
> To write on Angkor is a necessary part of the struggle for liberation.

Coming back from Indochina I was in Havana, Cuba, writing and directing a film. *Hjälparen; The Helper.* Not a film about Cuba. We only used Cuba as location. The film was about the international aid racket. Saving the poor of the world through experts on family planning, strawberry canning, modern puppet shows and once again family planning. (Getting their pay in hard currency. Having the diplomatic privileges of tax free liquor and imported cars to be sold on the black market.) We were working on a lean budget from the Swedish state television and the film was considered subversive even before the shooting began. Not even India would allow us to film it there. But that summer Cuba was in conflict not only with Washington but also with Moscow. They allowed us to work there and we could make a film that was not too bad. Anyway it was liked by the public and denounced by right-thinking editorialists.

We were to be on location at eight and in my hotel room I sat down at my Olivetti at four thirty every morning for three hours of writing. It was there in Havana I finished writing *Confessions of a Disloyal European.*

When I came to Sweden from Rome in December that year there were new antiwar demonstrations in Stockholm. Bigger than ever. The government issued orders for the police to break them up. I still have headaches from the beatings I got. I was arrested and the prosecutor wanted to put me in jail for up to four years for incitement to rebellion. But the demonstrations had become too large. The government reconsidered. If you can't beat them, join them! As 1968 began Olof Palme thus marched for the government in the front ranks of the now official mass antiwar demonstration.

Already this is as much history as when Peytel was among the young Republican heroes fighting for human and civic rights in the demonstrations at the barricades in rue Saint-Martin in June 1832.

But the world does move and we are not only blown down with the winds of change; we are the wind.

You could say that this book is an attempt to depict the European intellectual as a type. If I had written the book during the war in 1942 when I was fifteen I would—after listening to what Helge Ljung said about the European pre-Renaissance—have begun with the twelfth century free intellectuals, the wandering scholars, the vagantes and their Goliard songs.

When the War was over, the borders had begun to open and we sat around the bare wooden table at the auberge de la jeunesse in Avignon drinking the rough red wine and singing Bella Ciao, I thought about those comrades long gone who also did not allow themselves to sink and become just vagabonds or try to become right-thinking professors. Those who as their motto—omnia probate, try everything—had rephrased two of the more prudent works in 1 Thes. 5:21. "Prove all things; hold fast that which is good."

I am not sure later generations of European intellectuals now would identify with the vagantes as we did during the war. We, who now are their elders, have not given them that poetry as a refractory tradition. But as intellectuals their roots are still among the vagantes for better and for worse.